THE STRUCTURE AND MEANING OF BĀDARĀYAṆA'S BRAHMA SŪTRAS

THE STRUCTURE AND MEANING OF BĀDARĀYAṆA'S BRAHMA SŪTRAS

[A TRANSLATION AND ANALYSIS OF *ADHYĀYA* I]

GEORGE C. ADAMS, Jr.

MOTILAL BANARSIDASS PUBLISHERS
PRIVATE LIMITED • DELHI

First Edition: 1993

ISBN : 81-208-0931-9

Also available at
MOTILAL BANARSIDASS
Chowk, Varanasi 221 001
Ashok Rajpath, Patna 800 004
16 St Mark's Road, Bangalore 560 001
Bungalow Road, Jawahar Nagar, Delhi-110 007
120 Royapettah High Road, Mylapore, Madras 600 004

PRINTED IN INDIA
BY JAINENDRA PRAKASH JAIN AT SHRI JAINENDRA PRESS, A-45 NARAINA INDUSTRIAL AREA, PHASE I, NEW DELHI 110028 AND PUBLISHED BY NARENDRA PRAKASH JAIN FOR MOTILAL BANARSIDASS PUBLISHERS PVT. LTD., BUNGALOW ROAD, JAWAHAR NAGAR, DELHI 110007

To
My wife, Judy
and
Dr. Jose Pereira

Contents

I. INTRODUCTION
Importance of the *Brahma Sūtras* 1
Scope and Purpose 3

II. BACKGROUND OF THE *BRAHMA SŪTRAS*
Dating 7
Brahma Sūtras as *Uttara Mīmāṁsā* 9
Predecessors of Bādarāyaṇa 10
The Structure of the *Brahma Sūtras* 12
The *Sūtra* Style and Its Problems for the Modern Interpreter 13

III. IMPORTANT EXPOSITORS ON THE *BRAHMA SŪTRAS*
Introduction 19
Śaṅkara 19
Rāmānuja 23
Nimbārka 27
Vallabha 29
Madhva 31

IV. AN ANALYSIS OF THE *BRAHMA SŪTRAS* 1:1
Catuḥsūtrī: Introductory Aphorisms 37
Topic Five: Intelligibility 46
Topic Six: The Self Consisting of Joy 53
Topic Seven: The Solar Indweller 57
Topic Eight: Space 59
Topic Nine: Breath 60
Topic Ten: Light 60
Topic Eleven: Indra as Breath 62

V. AN ANALYSIS OF THE *BRAHMA SŪTRAS* 1:2
Topic One: The Being Consisting of Mind 67
Topic Two: The Eater 71

Topic Three: The Two Persons in the Cave 72
Topic Four: The Person within the Eye 73
Topic Five: The Inner Controller 75
Topic Six: The Invisible 78
Topic Seven: The Gastric Fire 79

VI. AN ANALYSIS OF THE *BRAHMA SŪTRAS* 1:3
Topic One: The Support of the Universe 87
Topic Two: The Abundance 88
Topic Three: The Imperishable 90
Topic Four: The Object of Seeing 92
Topic Five: The Small Space in the Heart 93
Topic Six: The Persons the Size of a Thumb 97
Topic Seven: The Deities as Students of the Vedas 98
Topic Eight: The *Śūdras* Inteligibility for Brahman Knowledge 101
Topic Nine: Breath 103
Topic Ten: Light 104
Topic Eleven: Space 104

VII. AN ANALYSIS OF THE *BRAHMA SŪTRAS* 1:4
Topic One: The Unmanifest 107
Topic Two: The Unborn 110
Topic Three: The Five Groups of Five 112
Topic Four: The Brahman as Creator 113
Topic Five: Whose Work is the World 114
Topic Six: The Self to be Seen, Heard, etc. 117
Topic Seven: The Material and Efficient Cause 120
Topic Eight: Closing 123

VIII. CONCLUSION
Preliminary Considerations 125
Bādarāyaṇa's Methodologies 126
The Theology of the *Brahma Sūtras:* Chapter One 128
The Theology of the *Brahma Sūtras:* A Summary of Chapter Two, Three, and Four 131
Closing Remarks 133

BIBLIOGRAPHY 135

APPENDICES
- A. A Comparison of *Adhikaraṇa* and *Sūtra* Breakdowns 139
- B. An Analysis of *Sūtra* Length 140
- C. Bādarāyaṇa's Methodology 141

INDEX 143

CHAPTER I

Introduction

IMPORTANCE OF THE BRAHMA SŪTRAS

The subject of this work, the *Brahma Sūtras*[1] (also known as the *Vedānta Sūtras*) of Bādarāyaṇa, holds a position of immense significance within both the Hindu tradition and the history of world religions.

Within the Hindu tradition, the significance of the *Sūtras* derives from the tremendous task that they purport to accomplish: summarizing and systematizing the teachings of revelation and, in particular, the Upaniṣads.[2] The Upaniṣads, of course, are the most important of the many Hindu religious scriptures. Consisting of a number of separate books, which in turn appear at times to be compilations from various sources, the Upaniṣads, dating from as early as 600 B.C., seek to set forth teachings on the nature of the supreme deity, the Brahman, and the relationship between the Brahman, the world, and the individual soul, or *jīva*. They do not represent a single, coherent system of thought, but rather contain a *variety* of views about the same basic themes. As Hume states,

> . . . the Upaniṣads are no homogeneous products, cogently presenting a philosophic theory, but they are compilations from different sources recording the 'guesses at truth' of the early Indians. A single, well articulated system cannot be deduced from them.[3]

Hence, we find in the Upaniṣads a wide variety of theological doctrines: Idealism and Realism; Difference, Identity, and Difference-in-Identity; devotion and gnosis; theism and impersonal monism; cosmologies identifying a variety of 'first causes': water, space, being, non-being, and personal Lord; and all of this presented in a variety of formats, including myths, rituals, hymns, and philosophical treatises.

The *Brahma Sūtras* attempted the intimidating task of systematizing this strange compilation of varied ideas expressed in varied forms, and identifying a consistent set of doctrines running throughout the Upaniṣads. From the apparent diversity of these scriptures, the *Brahma Sūtras* purported to bring forth a unity, in terms of a set of theological doctrines common to all the Upaniṣads, however differently they might be expressed from one Upaniṣad to another. Whether or not the *Brahma Sūtras* actually accomplish this task is open to debate (the *Sūtras*, for instance, address only a small number of Upaniṣadic passages), but in any case they have been *perceived* by Hindus as doing so, and hence held in high esteem.

The *Sūtras* were, in fact, held in such high esteem that no Hindu school of theology could expect serious recognition unless the school produced a commentary on the *Sūtras* demonstrating that its doctrines were consistent with those of the *Sūtras*. In order to achieve legitimacy, a new school would forego the difficult and complex task of proving its congruence with the multi-faceted Upaniṣads by focusing instead on the *Sūtras*, which provided a more orderly and concise summary of Upaniṣadic thought. Thus, the major Vedantic theologians—Śaṅkara, Rāmānuja, Nimbārka, Vallabha, and Madhva—all wrote commentaries on the *Brahma Sūtras*, demonstrating how their doctrines were consistent with the *Sūtras* of Bādarāyaṇa.[4] Indeed, the major work of each of these theologians was a commentary on the *Sūtras*.

The significance of the *Brahma Sūtras* for Hindu theology is thus twofold, for they not only summarized what came before them (i.e., the Upaniṣads) but also served as the basis of much that followed them (i.e., the Vedantic theologians). As Thibaut states of the *Brahma Sūtras*,

> they occupy a strictly central position, summarizing, on the one hand, a series of literary essays, extending over many generations, and forming, on the other hand, the head spring of an ever broadening activity of commentators as well as virtually independent writers, which reaches down to our days, and may yet have some future before itself.[5]

The significance of the *Brahma Sūtras* extends, however, beyond the realm of Hindu theology, for it is probable that they represent the first complete systematic theology, or at least the oldest systematic theology that has survived to our time, dating back to perhaps as early as the fifth century B.C.[6] While there are, of course, many religious writings, both within Hinduism and within other religious traditions, that are older than the *Brahma Sūtras*, these are either purported revelations found in the form of myth, hymn, ritual, and theological speculation or short theological works that are not of an all-encompassing and strictly systematic nature. The *Brahma Sūtras* are the oldest example of man's attempt to organize and systematize the unorganized body of revelation and discern a meaningful and consistent set of theological ideas out of revelation's apparent diversity. Bādarāyaṇa's work represents an early effort at accomplishing the same task that was to inspire theologians of all traditions for centuries, culminating perhaps in Catholic scholasticism: the urge to transform the complexity and diversity of revelation into the logic and unity of a systematic theology. Regardless of how well Bādarāyaṇa accomplished this task—and one can argue that he hardly formulated an exhaustive summary of Upaniṣadic doctrines—his significance in the history of theology remains merely because the *Sūtras* are our oldest example of systematic theology.

SCOPE AND PURPOSE

The *Brahma Sūtras* hold a somewhat paradoxical position in the history of theology, in that while on the one hand they have enjoyed considerable attention through the commentaries written on them by the Vedantic theologians, particularly Śaṅkara and Rāmānuja, on the other hand, as an *independent* work the *Sūtras* have received relatively little attention. They have served as the vehicle by which the systems of Rāmānuja, Śaṅkara, and others have been made known to the world, and particularly to Western readers, but while serving this role the *Sūtras* have been relatively neglected as an independent work. The magnificence and depth of the Vedantic commentaries have overshadowed the short, cryptic, and sometimes seemingly meaningless *sūtras* of Bādarāyaṇa.

In contrast, this work is devoted to the *Brahma Sūtras* as a work in itself. Our concern is not with what Śaṅkara, Rāmānuja, or other theologians have said *about* the *Brahma Sūtras*, but what the *Brahma Sūtras* themselves say. Our goal is to discern what Bādarāyaṇa actually meant, rather than what other Vedantic theologians *claim* he meant. While the Vedantic theologians will be referred to frequently, it will only be insofar as they help us shed light on the original meaning of the *Sūtras*.

There have, of course, been other works which have attempted to focus on Bādarāyaṇa's *Sūtras*, rather than on the commentators' interpretations of the *Sūtras*: in particular, the works of Radhakrishnan, Sharma, and Ghate come to mind. Each of these works, however, has a significant flaw which prevents it from being a definitive—and reliable—analysis of Bādarāyaṇa's thought. Radhakrishnan offers a lengthy, verse-by-verse description of all 555 *sūtras*; however, his analysis concentrates almost exclusively on the commentators' differing interpretations of the *Sūtras*, with little reference to Bādarāyaṇa's own meaning.[7] B.N.K. Sharma presents a lengthy and detailed analysis of the *Sūtras*, and devotes considerable attention to the question of the original meaning of the *Sūtras*. Unfortunately, Sharma writes as a devoted follower of Madhva's dualism, and his book—despite its excellent scholarship—amounts to little more than an eloquent defense of *Madhva's* interpretation of the *Sūtras*.[8] V.S. Ghate's *The Vedānta* presents an objective analysis of the *Sūtras* with reference to their original meaning, but does so in an unacceptably brief manner, covering the 555 *sūtras* in a mere one hundred pages.[9]

This work will attempt to combine the objectivity of Ghate with the thoroughness and detail of Sharma and Radhakrishnan, to arrive at a fair and non-biased assessment of what Bādarāyaṇa—not the commentators—meant when he composed the *Sūtras*. To do this, we will look at both the content and structure of the *Sūtras*—that is, we will look at not only the individual *sūtras*, but also the relationship between *sūtras*, as well as between *adhikaraṇas*, to find clues regarding their original meaning.

Unfortunately, given the vast nature of this task, limitations of time and space will require us to limit our analysis to the first, though in many ways the most important, *adhyāya*. This work therefore, should be seen as only a preliminary step setting a precedent and format for a complete analysis of the *Brahma Sūtras* which will examine all four *adhyāyas*.

FOOTNOTES

1. Where reference is made throughout the remainder of this work to 'the *Sūtras*', the reference is to the *Brahma Sūtras* of Bādarāyaṇa.

2. Of the major expositors on the *Brahma Sūtras*, Madhva more than anyone else emphasizes that the *Sūtras* summarize the teachings of all Vedic scriptures, including both *Śrūti* (Revelation) and *Smṛti* (Sacred Tradition).

3. David Hume, translator, *The Thirteen Principal Upaniṣads*, (London: Oxford University Press, 1971), p. 9. All translations of the Upaniṣads will be derived from Hume and Jose Pereira. The objective will be to provide readable, intelligible translations rather than literal translations. This same approach will be used in translating the *Sūtras*, where we will use free translations and insert Upaniṣadic passages where appropriate for the purpose of intelligibility.

4. Jose Pereira, *Hindu Theology: A Reader* (Garden City: Image Books, 1976), p. 239.

5. George Thibaut, translator, *The Vedānta Sūtras of Bādarāyaṇa with the Commentary of Śaṅkara*, Two vols. (New York: Dover, 1962; reprint of *Sacred Books of the East*, v. 38), 1:xii.

6. Pereira, *Hindu Theology*, p. 239.

7. S. Radhakrishnan, *The Brahma Sūtra: The Philosophy of Spiritual Life* (London: George Allen and Unwin, Ltd., 1960).

8. B.N.K. Sharma, *The Brahma Sūtras and Their Principal Commentaries* (Bombay: Bharatiya Vidya Bhavan, 1971), 3 vols.

9. V.S. Ghate, *The Vedānta: A Study of the Brahma Sūtras with the Bhaṣyas of Śaṅkara, Rāmānuja, Nimbārka, Madhva, and Vallabha* (Poona: Bhandarkar Oriental Research Institute, 1981).

CHAPTER II

Background of the *Brahma Sūtras*

DATING

While all scholars agree that the *Brahma Sūtras* represent one of the earliest works of systematic theology, there is some disagreement as to the precise dating of the work.

How one dates the *Brahma Sūtras* depends in part on what one sees the *Brahma Sūtras* to be a summary of. If, for instance, the *Sūtras* summarize only the Upaniṣads and scriptures preceding them, then the date of authorship must be considerably earlier than if the *Sūtras* summarize the Upaniṣads and other Smṛti writings, many of which, of course, were written later than the Upaniṣads. B.N.K. Sharma, for instance, argues for a later dating of the *Brahma Sūtras* on the grounds that they summarize not only the Upaniṣads, but also the post-Vedic writings such as Smṛtis, Itihāsas, and Purāṇas. To support his position, Sharma claims that the *Brahma Sūtras* are referred to in the *Bhagavad Gītā* in Chapter 13, verse 4:

> *ṛṣibhir bahudhā gītam chandobhir vividhaiḥ pṛthak brahma-sūtrapadaiś caiva hetumadbhir viniścitaiḥ*
> ('In many ways has it been sung by seers, in varied hymns each in its separate way, in aphoristic verses concerning the Brahman, well reasoned and conclusive.')[1]

Edgerton and Zaehner, however, both doubt that the *Gītā* refers to the *Brahma Sūtras*. Zaehner, for instance, points out that while the *Gītā* includes references to Sāṅkhya and Yoga principles, the *Sāṅkhya-kārikā* and *Yoga-sūtras* were most likely written after the *Gītā*, and likewise the *Gītā* could refer to aphoristic statements about the Brahman without necessarily referring to the specific collection of aphorisms authored by Bādarāyaṇa. Neither Zaehner nor Edgerton, however, offer any extensive argument in favour of their contention that the *Brahma Sūtras* are not referred to in the *Gītā*, and hence they are of little help in determining its date.[2] It should be noted, however, that in support of the contention that the *Gītā* does indeed refer to the *Brahma Sūtras* of Bādarāyaṇa, there is no evidence to suggest that anyone preceded Bādarāyaṇa in authoring a set of *sūtras* on the Brahman that were 'well reasoned and conclusive,' as the *Gītā* describes them.

Damodar Garge takes a different approach to dating the *Brahma Sūtras* by focusing on the fact that Bādarāyaṇa and Jaimini, author of the *Mīmāṃsā Sūtras*, are mentioned in each other's works, and hence were roughly contemporaneous. Jaimini mentions Bādarāyaṇa in five *sūtras* (1.1.5, 5.2.19, 6.1.8, 10.8.44, and 11.1.63); Bādarāyaṇa refers to Jaimini on ten occasions (1.2.28, 1.2.31, 1.3.31, 3.2.40, 3.4.2, 3.4.18, 3.4.40, 4.3.12, 4.4.5, and 4.4.11). Of course, Garge has no way of conclusively demonstrating that the Bādarāyaṇa referred to by Jaimini is the Bādarāyaṇa who authored the *Brahma Sūtras*, or that the Jaimini referred to by Bādarāyaṇa is the author of the *Mīmāṃsā Sūtras*. Garge's main piece of evidence is a statement by Sureśvara that Jaimini, author of the *Mīmāṃsā Sūtras*, was also a Vedāntin who composed his own *Vedānta Sūtras*, the first two of which are identical to those of Bādarāyaṇa. One could also interpret Bādarāyaṇa's first *sūtra*, beginning with the famous and controversial '*Athāto*' ('Then, therefore'), as implying that the *Brahma Sūtras* were preceded by another work, which logically could have been *Mīmāṃsā sūtras*, in accordance with the Vedāntic tradition that the study of ritual (*Mīmāṃsā*) precedes the study of knowledge (*Vedānta*), although this would not necessarily prove that Bādarāyaṇa was a contemporary of Jaimini.[3]

Nonetheless, on the other hand there is no evidence to indicate that there were any 'Bādarāyaṇa's' or 'Jaimini's' other than those who authored the *Brahma Sūtras* and *Mīmāṃsā Sūtras*. Hindu tradition refers only to these two specific theologians, consistently identifies them with the same two major works, and unanimously proclaims Jaimini to have been the pupil of Bādarāyaṇa.

The specific dating, therefore, of the *Brahma Sūtras*, remains uncertain. Garge, assuming that Bādarāyaṇa and Jaimini were contemporaries and that Jaimini lived in the *Śrautasūtra* period, argues for the earliest authorship of the *Sūtras* at sometime around 500 B.C.[4] At the other extreme, we have Jacobi estimating authorship at between 200 and 450 A.D., while in between there is Das Gupta's estimate of 200 B.C. and Radhakrishnan's estimate of the fourth century B.C.[5] Perhaps the only conclusive remark that can be made is that while the precise date of the *Brahma Sūtras* is uncertain, and the subject of considerable disagreement, all agree that it represents one of the earliest attempts at systematizing the unsystematic contents of a body of scripture, and, as such, holds a unique position in the history of theology regardless of its exact date of authorship.

BRAHMA SŪTRAS AS UTTARA MĪMĀṂSĀ

The Hindu scriptural tradition is quite remarkable for its size and diversity: not only are there a very large number of works designated as revelation, but the specific content of these works varies greatly. In order to make this vast body of literature more manageable, it was necessary for theologians to summarize and reconcile the many different theological doctrines found in scripture. Within the Hindu tradition, this task developed into a separate field of theological writing, known as *mīmāṃsā*. Thibaut defines *mīmāṃsā* as the 'investigation or inquiry into the connected meaning of the sacred texts', or more extensively:

> the task of taking a comprehensive view of the Vedic writings as a whole, of systematizing what they present in an unsystematical form, of showing the mutual coordination or subordination of single passages and sections, and of reconciling contradictions.[6]

The *mīmāṃsā* tradition developed along two lines that stand out in varying degrees of conflict and conformity throughout the Hindu tradition, namely the distinction between *karma* (or *dharma*) and *jñāna*, or action and knowledge as the means of liberation. The action or works tradition (*karmakāṇḍa*) focused on adherence to the Brahmanical sacrifices and rules for ritual and social conduct as the path to salvation. From this tradition came two *mīmāṃsā*-type works, the *Kalpa Sūtras*, which were concise descriptions of the Brahmanical sacrifices, and the *Pūrva Mīmāṃsā Sūtras*, which summarized the doctrines and principles behind the sacrificial tradition. The *Pūrva Mīmāṃsā* tradition drew largely from the Brahmaṇas and Saṁhitās, and included such notable figures as Jaimini, Śabara, Kumārila Bhaṭṭa, and Prabhākara, the most important of which was Jaimini, whose *Pūrva Mīmāṃsā Sūtras* parallels Bādarāyaṇa's *Brahma Sūtras*.[7]

In contrast with the *Pūrva Mīmāṃsā* tradition stood the parallel *Uttara Mīmāṃsā* tradition which summarized those Hindu scriptures which focused on knowledge rather than works, as the means to salvation. *Uttara Mīmāṃsā* represented a systematization of *jñāna-kāṇḍa*, and drew its texts primarily from the Upaniṣads and Āraṇyaka portion of the Brāhmaṇas.[8] Presumably there were many authors of *Uttara Mīmāṃsā* works, although Bādarāyaṇa's has assumed the greatest historical importance in terms of its influence on other theologians down the ages, and hence stands as the *Uttara Mīmāṃsā* counterpart to Jaimini's *Pūrva Mīmāṃsā Sūtras*, the outstanding work of the genre.[9]

Inasmuch as the sacrificial and ritual scriptures tend to predate the scriptures that focus on knowledge, and because ritual is viewed as a preparation for the study of the Brahman, the summaries of the sacrificial and ritual texts are designated '*pūrva*' or 'early' *mīmāṃsā*, and the knowledge summaries '*uttara*' or 'later' *mīmāṃsā*. The specific relationship between these two genres (e.g., must study of *Pūrva Mīmāṃsā* precede study of *Uttara Mīmāṃsā*?) is a point hotly debated between the various commentators on the *Brahma Sūtras*.[10]

PREDECESSORS OF BĀDARĀYAṆA

While Bādarāyaṇa's *Brahma Sūtras* became the most significant systematic summary of Vedantic thought—significant, that is, in terms of influence on the development of Hindu theology—and also the only extant work in its genre, most scholars tend to assume that Bādarāyaṇa was part of a larger tradition of *Uttara Mīmāṃsā* works that preceded his own work, just as numerous other theologians developed the *Pūrva Mīmāṃsā* tradition prior to its culmination in Jaimini. As the crowning achievement of *Uttara Mīmāṃsā*, Bādarāyaṇa's *Brahma Sūtra* has not only survived but actually grown in stature while the works of his predecessors have disappeared.

Unfortunately, given that there are no extant works by Bādarāyaṇa's predecessors, we are left without concrete proof that Bādarāyaṇa's work was part of a larger tradition rather than an isolated and unique work. Logic, of course, would dictate that given the conflicting realities in early Hindu thought between a multiplicity of scriptures on the one hand and a spiritual quest for unity and oneness on the other hand, efforts at unifying the scriptures would be commonplace. That a culture oriented toward a unitary vision of the universe would tacitly accept revelations that lacked unity would simply not make sense.

In terms of actual evidence to support this apparently logical assumption that Bādarāyaṇa had predecessors in the task of systematizing Vedantic thought, scholars point to internal evidence within the *Brahma Sūtras* itself, specifically, to Bādarāyaṇa's references to teachers other than himself. Eight teachers are mentioned by Bādarāyaṇa, some in agreement with him, some not:[11]

1. Ātreya: 3.4.44
2. Āśmarathya: 1.2.29, 1.4.20
3. Auḍulomi: 1.4.21, 3.4.45, 4.4.6
4. Kārṣṇājini: 3.1.9
5. Kāśakṛtsna: 1.4.22
6. Jaimini: 1.2.28.31, 1.3.31
7. Bādari: 1.2.30
8. Bādarāyaṇa: 1.3.26, 1.3.33.

However, while Bādarāyaṇa's references to these theologians provide substantiation that thinkers other than himself pondered the meaning of Vedantic texts, these references do not in any way demonstrate the existence of a tradition of Vedanta-based systematic theology preceding his own *Brahma Sūtras*. There is, for instance, no proof that the theologians referred to by Bādarāyaṇa were his *predecessors* rather than *contemporaries*. Madhva, in fact, argues that the individuals alluded to by Bādarāyaṇa were his *disciples* whom he referred to for the sake of giving them publicity![12] Furthermore, even if we assume that these thinkers were predecessors to Bādarāyaṇa, there is no evidence to indicate that, like Bādarāyaṇa, they attempted to systematize the entire corpus of Vedantic scripture: could they not have been thinkers who wrote on isolated, specific questions without attempting to unify their thought into a systematic whole?

The answers, of course, to these questions cannot be determined. While it can be assumed that theologians other than Bādarāyaṇa were attracted to the task of systematizing the Vedantic scriptures, we cannot know to what extent any of them approached the completeness and breadth of Bādarāyaṇa's work, all of which perhaps justifies the statement that 'Systematic theology can be said to have emerged from his (Bādarāyaṇa's) head as Athena from that of Zeus.'[13]

THE STRUCTURE OF THE BRAHMA SŪTRAS

The stature in which Bādarāyaṇa's work is held is based on the twofold greatness of the work: that is, greatness in both content and form. As indicated above, the *Sūtras'* content is outstanding in that it represents the first comprehensive treatment in a systematic manner of the vast corpus of Vedic thought. However, the *Sūtras* are also outstanding in the *form* by which that content is expressed. Bādarāyaṇa takes a vast body of scripture and organizes it into an exquisite work of order and symmetry that at least gives the appearance of bringing order into the disorder of the multitude of different Upaniṣadic speculations.

The largest division of the work is into four main chapters, or *adhyāyas*. There is universal agreement among all commentators that Bādarāyaṇa divided his work into these four main chapters. The first two chapters deal with the Brahman as He is in Himself, the last two with the Brahman as the goal of human existence. More specifically, the first chapter is classified as *Samanvaya*, or Order, and attempts to reconcile the different Upaniṣadic doctrines on the nature of the Brahman. The second chapter, *Avirodha*, or Concord, shows how apparently contradictory doctrines can be reconciled, and how the Vedantic philosophy withstands the challenges of other schools of thought. Chapter three, *Sādhanā* or *Mārga*, deals with 'Way', or means of liberation, and chapter four, *Phalam*, or Fruit, focuses on the nature of liberation and attainment of the Brahman.[14]

From the *adhyāyas*, Bādarāyaṇa extends the symmetry of the *Sūtras* even further by dividing each chapter into four sections, or *pādas*. As with the *adhyāyas*, all commentators agree in dividing the work into four *pādas* per *adhyāya*, or a total of sixteen *pādas*.

Each *pāda* is further divided into a series of topics, or *adhikaraṇas*, each of which is composed of several *sūtras*, or brief sentences. The *adhikaraṇas* are often arranged in a systematic manner, with one topic logically leading to the next. Each *adhikaraṇa* was based on a particular text of revelation, known as the *viṣaya vākya*, or 'topical text'. The *sūtras* comprising each *adhikaraṇa* were devoted to explaining the intent of the topical text. Among the major commentators, there is close but not complete agreement regarding the number of *adhikaraṇas* composing each *pāda*, and the number of *sūtras* composing each *adhikaraṇa*. Śaṅkara, for instance, identifies 191 *adhikaraṇas* and 555 *sūtras*, while Madhva identifies 223 *adhikaraṇas* and 563 *sūtras* (see Appendix A for a more detailed breakdown).

With this division into *adhyāyas*, *pādas*, *adhikaraṇas*, and *sūtras*, the *Brahma Sūtras* can be seen as a work in which content was presented in accordance with a specific form, thereby imposing some order on the vast body of Vedic literature. While the commentators disagree on the precise division of the *Brahma Sūtras*' form, all agree that it is a work of exceptional order and symmetry.

THE SŪTRA STYLE AND ITS PROBLEM FOR THE MODERN INTERPRETER

In any attempt to determine the original meaning of Bādarāyaṇa's *Brahma Sūtras*, the primary focus must be on the individual *sūtras*—approximately 555 in all, the number depending on the expositor—for only if their individual meaning can be established is it possible to accurately draw conclusions based on the structure formed by the inter-relatedness of the individual *sūtras*. Unfortunately, the nature of the *sūtras* is such that in many cases their original meaning cannot be determined with much certainty.

The interpretative problems posed by the *sūtra* style are several. Perhaps the most difficult problem is posed by the very nature of the *sūtras*, which aim at *conciseness* above all else. A *sūtra* is sort of a 'bare bones' sentence, containing only the essential, key words that are necessary to communicate a given thought. In short, the purpose of the *sūtra* is to communicate as much as possible in as few words as possible. The *sūtras* are therefore sparse and lean, devoid of unnecessary verbiage and wordiness. Thibaut's description of the *sūtra* style is quite appropriate:

> All *sūtras* aim at conciseness; that is clearly the reason to which this whole species of literary composition owes its existence. Thus their aim they reach by the rigid exclusion of all words which can possibly be spared, by the careful avoidance of all unnecessary repetition.... At the same time the manifest intention of the *sūtra* writers is to express themselves with as much clearness as the conciseness affected by them admits of. The aphorisms are indeed often concise to excess, but not otherwise intentionally obscure, the manifest care of the writers being to sacrifice only what can be supplied, although perhaps not without difficulty, and an irksome strain of memory and reflection.[15]

Why, it might be asked, would ideas of such importance be expressed in a manner so open to misinterpretation? The answer to this question lies in the fact that the written *sūtras* were only guidelines to unwritten thoughts that were much more comprehensive than the written *sūtras*. The words of the written *sūtra* represented only the key words of the thought behind the written words. As such, the written *sūtra* functioned to trigger a series of associated words committed only to memory. Literally, '*sūtra*' means 'thread' or 'string': in essence the words of the *sūtra* functioned as the thread or string which connected the ideas committed only to memory.

That important theological speculation should be committed to memory rather than writing might seem rather odd to the Western mind. Such a practice, however, had roots in the Indic understanding of the nature of truth and its communication to man. The Vedic tradition viewed truth as 'subsisting eternally as subtle sound',[16] and being transmitted to man by being *heard* (*Śrutra*) by sages, who committed these truth/sounds to memory. Truth, in other words, was not just an idea or concept, but a particular *sound* as well. Given this understanding of truth, it follows that *writing* could not serve as an adequate medium for the expression of truth since the element of sound was not present in writing. Hence, as Pereira puts it, writing was regarded as 'an unworthy vehicle for the transmission of sacred knowledge.'[17]

The net effect of the *sūtra* style's conciseness is that the translator is often required to fill in words in order to create a meaningful translation.

The very first *sūtra*, for instance, reads *athāto brahmajijñāsā*. Literally, this translates into 'Now (*atha*) therefore (*atas*), Brahman inquiry (*Brahmajiñāsā*).' To make a sensible translation we must add a verb which is absent in the Sanskrit *sūtra*: 'Now, therefore, we begin the inquiry into the Brahman.' Even with this translation, however, the *sūtra* remains ambiguous since we do not know what the 'Now, therefore' refers to. Presumably it is a referent to something which must precede the inquiry into the Brahman. While this is generally understood to mean the *Pūrva Mīmāṃsā*, or inquiry into ritual, the *sūtra* itself does not say so. Furthermore, even if we acknowledge that the *sūtra* speaks with reference to *Pūrva Mīmāṃsā* as that which precedes the inquiry into the Brahman, the *sūtra* says nothing about the precise nature of the relationship between the Brahman-inquiry and the works-inquiry that precedes it. For instance, is the inquiry into works a necessary or optional prerequisite to the inquiry into the Brahman? When the *sūtra* says that '*Now* then is the inquiry into the Brahman', does it mean to imply that the inquiry into works must have preceded? The *sūtra* simply does not answer this question, leaving open an opportunity for commentators to insert their own views, which, for instance, Śaṅkara and Rāmānuja do at considerable length.

The second *sūtra* (1.1.2) provides another illustration of the problems presented by the *sūtras*' conciseness. Literally, it reads: '*Janmādyasya Yataḥ*,' or 'The origin, etc., of this from which.' Fortunately, all commentators agree that the meaning of this *sūtra* is something to the effect of, 'That from which comes the origin, preservation, and dissolution of this world is the Brahman.' Note that the words of the *sūtra* do not even contain the subject of the sentence (Brahman), nor do they state that '*asya*' refers to the world: in other words, the two key words without which the *sūtra* would not make sense are excluded and must be inserted by the commentator/translator.

In these two examples where key words are not included in the *sūtra*, there is general agreement among commentators regarding what words should be inserted. However, this is certainly not always the case, as can be seen, for example, in *sūtra* 1.1.5: *īkṣaternāśabdam*. This can be broken down into: *īkṣater* (on account of knowing or seeing), *na* (not), and *aśabdam* (not expressible; not Vedic or scriptural).

Part of the difficulty in interpreting this *sūtra*—a difficulty encountered in many of Bādarāyaṇa's *sūtras*—is the uncertainty regarding the *subject* of the sentence. Rāmānuja and Śaṅkara, for instance, take *aśabdam* as the subject, and interpret it as referring to the Sāṅkhya *pradhāna*, or Prime Matter which the Sāṇkhyas hold to be the origin of the world. *Pradhāna* is derived from the *sūtra's aśabdam* on the grounds that it is 'not founded in Scripture', but rather on reason. Rāmānuja and Śaṅkara interpret *na* as referring to that which is the origin, etc., of the world, as first referred to in 1.1.2. (*janmādyasya*): *na* establishes that 'that which is not founded on Scripture' (or *Pradhāna*) is not the origin, etc., of the world. Finally, *īkṣater* is interpreted as providing the *reason* for affirming that *Pradhāna* is not the origin of the world: because of the word 'seeing' (found in the *viṣaya vākya* that speaks of creation) being associated with that which is the origin of the world, that origin cannot be *Pradhāna* since *Pradhāna* is an impersonal entity which lacks such qualities as 'seeing'. Hence, as a final interpretation of the *sūtra* we have,

> That which is not founded on Scripture (*Pradhāna*) is not the origin of the world because of the reference to 'seeing'.

This is a logical interpretation of the three words of Bādarāyaṇa's *sūtra*, but it is certainly not the *only* logical interpretation. Madhva, for instance, inserts 'Brahman' as the topic of the sentence, and views *aśabdam* as a description of the Brahman. Specifically, he states that 'the Brahman is not inexpressible (*aśabdam*) becasue he is an object of knowledge (*īkṣater*)'—as indicated in the *viṣaya vākya* text.[18]

One can, of course, argue for the validity of one or other interpretations of this *sūtra*, but our point here is not to make such a judgment, but rather to point out how the brevity and conciseness of Bādarāyaṇa's *sūtras* leave them open to a variety of logical interpretations.

The conciseness of the *sūtras* is not the only problem encountered by the interpreter, however. The Sanskrit language in itself is of such a nature that precise translation is a difficult task since the meaning of words and groupings of words in compounds is often obscure. Pereira describes the challenges presented by the language quite well:

> To begin with, the syntax of Sanskrit—with its inordinate love of nouns and adjectival compounds, and its near aversion to verbs—is wholly dissimilar to that of any language known in the modern West. This intimidates translators, as do some of the language's other peculiarities. Among them is an inflectional intricacy that permits the creation of composite words—words succinctly encapsuling ideas of a richness of nuance that tongues of a lighter digestion (such as English) can assimilate only with difficulty, or not at all. Another peculiarity is its phenomenal capacity for abbreviation, combined with a contrary penchant for diffuseness and ornamentation—the latter propensity being further stimulated by the language's luxuriance of synonyms.[59]

Yet another problem encountered in the search for the true meanings of Bādarāyaṇa's *Sūtras* is that of the *viṣaya vākya*, or topical texts. Each *sūtra* (or series of *sūtras*) is based on a passage in revelation. Unfortunately, Bādarāyaṇa does not indicate what passages his *sūtras* refer to, the result being that in the some *sūtras* the meaning is not apparent since it can only be understood with reference to the Scriptural passage to which it refers. Likewise, in some *sūtras* the meaning can be manipulated according to which *viṣaya vākya* one contends that the *sūtra* refers to. Śaṅkara and Rāmānuja, for instance, interpret the important *īkṣatyadhikaraṇa* on the basis of it referring to *Chāndogya Upaniṣad* 6:2:3, while Madhva offers a much different interpretation of the same *adhikaraṇa* based on the assumption that the *sūtra* derives from several *viṣaya vākyas*, from the *Bṛhadāraṇyaka*, *Praśna*, and *Kaṭha* Upaniṣads, the *Ṛg Veda*, and the *Pravṛtta Saṁhitā*.[20]

To summarize, three factors stand in the way of any attempt to determine the original meaning of the *Brahma Sūtras:* the *sūtra* style itself, the Sanskrit language, and the *viṣaya vākyas*. These factors place significant limits on the *accuracy* with which we can speculate on the *Sūtra's* original meaning. At the same time, however, these factors demonstrate the importance of looking at the structure or interrelatedness of the *Sūtras*, since the manner in which a given *sūtra* fits in with *other sūtras* can sometimes be a clue to its meaning. *Where* a *sūtra* is placed sometimes can provide a clue to *what* it means.[21]

FOOTNOTES

1. B.N.K. Sharma, *Brahma Sūtras*, 1:2.
2. See R.C. Zaehner, *The Bhagavad Gītā* (London: Oxford University Harvard University Press, 1972).
3. Damodar Garge, *Citations in Śabara Bhaṣya* (Poona: Deccan College, 1952), pp. 14–15
4. Garge, *Citations in Śabara Bhaṣya*, p. 17.
5. See Surendranath Das Gupta, *A History of Indian Philosophy*, 5 vols. (Cambridge; University Press, 1949), 1:370; Radhakrishnan, *Brahma Sūtras*, p. 22, and Radhakrishnan, *Indian Philosophy*, 2 vols. (New York: MacMillan and Co. 1927) 2:376.
6. Thibaut, trans., *Vedānta Sūtras with Commentary of Śaṅkara*, 1:ix.
7. Das Gupta, *History of Indian Philosophy*, 1:69.
8. Thibaut, trans., *Vedānta Sūtras with Commentary of Śaṅkara*, 1:ix–x.
9. Thus, the derivation of the various *sūtra* writings from revelation can be diagrammed as follows:

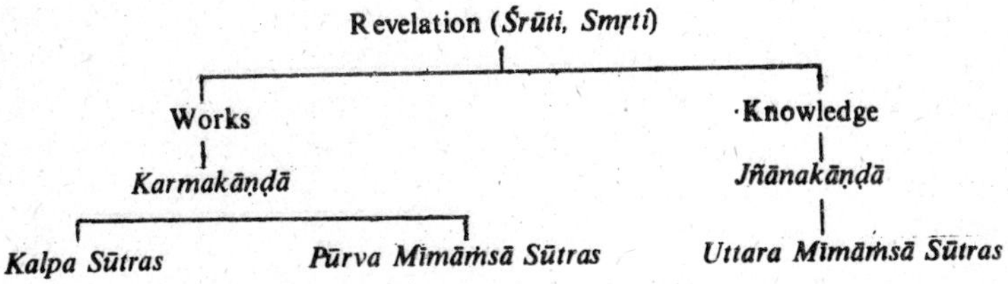

10. See, for instance, the commentaries by Śaṅkara and Rāmānuja on *Brahma Sūtra* 1.1.1, where the words *atha* and *atas* generate extensive discussion over the relationship between works and knowledge.

11. Radhakrishnan, *Brahma Sūtras*, p. 22.

12. B.N.K. Sharma, *Brahma Sūtras*, 1:1.

13. Jose Pereira, 'Bādarāyaṇa: Creator of Systematic Theology'. *Religious Studies* 22, (Feb., 1987): 199.

14. Pereira, 'Bādarāyaṇa', p. 195.

15. Thibaut, trans., *Vedāanta Sūtras with Commentary by Śaṅkara*, 1: xiii. Also see Śabara's remarks on the sūtra style in Pereira, *Hindu Theology*, p. 89.

16. Pereira, 'Bādarāyaṇa', p. 197.

17. Ibid. Of course, this idea is not unique to Indic thought. Both the Druids and the priests of the Greek mystery religions refused to commit their teachings to written form.

18. For a further analysis of this *sūtra*, see below, Chapter IV, pp. 67–70.

19. Pereira, *Hindu Theology*, pp. 17–18.

20. B.N.K. Sharma, *Brahma Sūtras*, 1:86–95.

21. Thus, for example, as we shall argue below, the placement of a *sūtra*, describing the Brahman as creator of the world, at the very beginning of the *Brahma Sūtras* (1.1.2), provides rather strong evidence that Bādarāyaṇa perceived this to be an essential quality of the Brahman, and from this we can deduce that Bādarāyaṇa's theology advocates a realism in which creator and created world both exist—a position that is congruent with the thought of Rāmānuja, Madhva, and other Realists, but in conflict with the Idealism of Śaṅkara.

CHAPTER III

Important Expositors on the *Brahma Sūtras*

INTRODUCTION

The focus of this work is to examine the *Brahma Sūtras* for the purpose of exploring what Bādarāyaṇa meant when the authored them: we are not attempting any type of comparative analysis of how the major expositors *interpreted* Bādarāyaṇa's *Sūtras.*[1] Nonetheless, a familiarity with the interpretations of the major expositors is a necessary part of our analysis, since it is only through their interpretations that we can begin to make sense of the *Sūtras.* Without the expositors' interpretations, we are left with a series of cryptic and apparently meaningless phrases. Only with the assistance of the expositors can we begin to piece together word to word, *sūtra* to *sūtra*, and *adhikaraṇa* to *adhikaraṇa.* Granted that the expositors' interpretations of the *sūtras* are biased, if we are familiar with their systems we can make an attempt to identify how and where these biases effect their interpretations, and hence separate the expositors' bias from the *sūtrakāra's* original intent.

It is not the intent of this work to examine all of the expositors on the *Brahma Sūtras.* While Sharma identifies twenty-one pre-Madhva commentaries on the *Sūtras,*[2] more commonly we see reference to twelve such authors: Śaṅkara, Bhāskara, Yādavaprakāśa, Rāmānuja, Madhva, Nimbārka, Srīkaṇṭha, Śrīpati, Vallabha, Śuka, Vijñānabhikṣu, and Baladeva.[3]

For our purpose, however, we shall limit our discussion of the expositors to the five most prominent ones: the monists, Śaṅkara and Vallabha; the Difference-in-Identity theologians, Rāmānuja and Nimbārka; and the Dualist, Madhva.

ŚAṄKARA

In Śaṅkara we have perhaps the most widely known interpretation of Vedantic theology, an interpretation that sometimes is erroneously identified as being *synonymous* with Vedanta rather than just one among many different interpretations of Vedantic thought.

Of the five expositors that we shall examine, Śaṅkara is the earliest, living in the late eighth and early ninth centuries (788 to 820 A.D.). While generally identified as the *founder* of a school of thought, he actually was more like the outstanding spokesman for a larger school of thought which included predecessors, such as Gauḍapāda and Govinda.[4]

Śaṅkara's system is identified as *kevalādvaita*, or absolute non-dualism. Śaṅkara's position purports to be monism in its purest form, asserting that ultimately there is only one undifferentiated reality without any semblance of difference or distinction, real at all times, past, present and future. The world of multiplicity which is perceived through human senses is transitory reality or illusion, and this illusion becomes apparent to the man of knowledge who comes to understand that all difference is an appearance only, obscuring the one, true, non-dual reality.

In accordance with the Vedantic categories, Śaṅkara identifies this reality as the Brahman. The Brahman alone is real, while the world of souls and matter, characterized as they are by difference, are illusory. The nature of the Brahman is that of pure intelligence, since he is described as such in the Upaniṣads. He is not a 'knower', however, since the act of knowing implies a distinction between the knower and that which is known, thereby establishing a duality.

Likewise, the Brahman does not possess qualities, since the presence of a quality can only be discerned if there exists some type of distinction between the quality and that which is qualified. Take, for example, the case of a blue lily. The quality 'blue' must somehow be different from 'lily', since otherwise the connection of the two words would not convey a meaning different from the mere word 'lily'. This, of course, is not the case since 'blue lily' clearly conveys a different meaning than 'lily'. With regard to the Brahman, this means, for instance, that He is not an intelligent being—i.e., a being qualified by intelligence—but rather pure intelligence in and of itself. Intelligence is the very substance of the Brahman, not just an attribute of Him.[5]

Śaṅkara's absolute non-dualism forces him to adopt the *vivarta* view of causation, according to which there is no difference between cause and effect, with the effects only *appearing* to be different from the cause. This contrasts with the *pariṇāma*, or transformationist doctrine which sees the effect as a real transformation of the cause. As applied to the relationship between the Brahman and the world, the *vivarta* doctrine holds that only the Brahman as the cause is real, while the created world, as the effect, is illusory.

Śaṅkara's doctrine of absolute non-dualism presents a number of theological dilemmas, one of the most significant of which is how to explain our perception of difference if such difference does not even exist. If all reality is one, how is it possible for difference to be perceived, or how is it possible for perception to occur at all unless there exists both the perceiver and the object perceived, hence creating a duality?

Śaṅkara attempts to solve this problem through his doctrine of *māyā*, a doctrine that offers an explanation of the perception of multiplicity only at the expense of introducing new theological dilemmas. *Māyā* is often used synonymously with *avidyā*, and is best understood as misperception, ignorance of the true nature of things, or wrong knowledge. Śaṅkara unfortunately fails to clearly define the precise ontological status of *māyā*, stating that it is neither existent (*sat*) nor non-existent (*asat*), since if existent it would posit a reality in addition to the Brahman, thereby destroying non-duality; yet if non-existent it therefore could not exercise *any* impact on the world and hence could not account for the perception of multiplicity. However ambiguous, Thibaut's description of *māyā* is perhaps as precise as we can get: 'the *undefinable cause* owing to which there seems to exist a material world comprehending distinct individual existences.'[6] At times Śaṅkara associates *māyā* with the Brahman as one of His powers: just as the magician has the magical power to make a rope *appear* to be a snake, so the Brahman has the power to make the world *appear* to be multifold rather than one, an act He engages in for the purposes of creation and making Himself accessible to his devotees.

This, of course, presents a number of dilemmas since if there is only one non-dual reality, to whom or what is the illusion presented, and if the Brahman is truly one, how can an illusion—which by definition is different from His true nature—exist at all?

Śaṅkara's absolute non-dualism poses further problems: if there is only the one non-dual Brahman, then how can the Vedic revelation have meaning, since it presupposes a difference between seeker and that which is sought, between worshipper and object of worship? Śaṅkara responds to this challenge by positing two levels of truth along with two aspects of the Brahman. The teachings on devotion, worship, and works which posit a distinction between man and personal God, full of auspicious qualities, are written at a lower level of truth (*vyāvahārika*), designed for individuals who are not yet capable of understanding the higher level of truth (*pāramārthika*), where only the one non-dual Brahman is perceived as real and all else—including the individual self—is recognized as illusory. The personal Lord and the religious injunctions pertaining to his worship are thus part of a lower—and ultimately false—level of knowledge that is abandoned once the non-dual nature of reality is recognised.[7]

Concerning the means by which man acquires true knowledge of the Brahman, two points of Śaṅkara's thought are worth noting. First, Śaṅkara declares that knowledge is gained through direct experience (*anubhava*) of the Brahman, as opposed to mere rational understanding of Him through the use of reason (*tarka*). Reason, along with revelation (*Śrūti*), can help man achieve a clearer understanding of the nature of the Brahman, but only direct experience of the Brahman yields final liberation and a cessation of the illusory perception of difference and multiplicity.[8]

Secondly, Śaṅkara argues—in contrast to most of the other Vedantic theologians—that knowledge of and performance of religious works (*dharma*) is not a prerequisite to obtaining knowledge of the Brahman and its accompanying liberation. Rather, man can enter directly into the quest for the Brahman knowledge without having first completed the many rites and practices as prescribed by the Vedas.[9]

It is interesting to note, however, that the very concept of man attaining knowledge of the Brahman would seem to be invalidated by the ontological presuppositions of Śaṅkara's system. If all reality is one, and that reality is the Brahman, who or what can engage in an inquiry and search, since such an activity can only occur if there exists a *difference* between seeker and object sought? Śaṅkara, of course, takes note of this dilemma and attempts to respond to it in his commentary on the *Brahma Sūtras*.

> But if the Brahman is generally known as the Self, there is no room for an inquiry into it. Not so, we reply; for there is a conflict of opinions as to its special nature.[10]

This answer, however, fails to adequately respond to the question since the existence of conflicting opinions—indeed, the existence of any opinions or even the beings who hold those opinions—implies a duality that is not compatible with Śaṅkara's assertion of absolute non-dualism.

RĀMĀNUJA

Rāmānuja (ca. 1017 to 1127) ranks as the most prominent member of the *viśiṣta-advaita*, or Qualified Nondualism school of Vedantic thought. In contrast to Śaṅkara, who though in practice was a devout Hindu, tended to separate religion from theology in his writings, the Qualified Nondualism school attempted to combine the rigorous logic and structure of Vedantic theology with the fervor and intensity of their Vaiṣṇava religion. Hence, as Pereira states:

> Qualified Nondualism is an event of great moment in Hindu theology. On the one hand were the theologies of knowledge, developed to the highest imaginable point of sophistication; on the other, the ebullient newer trend of devotion, clamouring for theological synthesis. It was Qualified Nondualism that combined the architectonics of the one with the fieriness of the other, thus becoming the first Vedantic theology of devotion.[11]

Just as Śaṅkara was preceded by a number of earlier non-dualist theologians, likewise Rāmānuja was preceded by several Vaiṣṇava theologians who advocated Qualified Nondualism. Most prominent perhaps was Rāmānuja's own teacher, Yāmuna, but even preceding him were such notables as Taṅka, Dramiḍa, and Bodhāyana.

Rāmānuja's thought is embodied in four principal works: the *Śrībhāṣya*, his magnum opus commentary on the *Brahma Sūtras*; the *Gītābhāṣya*, a commentary on the *Bhagavad Gītā*; and two shorter Vedantic treatises, the *Vedārthasaṁgraha* and the *Vedāntadīpa*.

As indicated above, Rāmānuja's theology is based on *viśiṣṭādvaita*, or Qualified Nondualism, in contrast to the unqualified or Pure non-dualism of Śaṅkara. To Rāmānuja, the non-dual nature of reality is qualified in the sense that, unlike Śaṅkara's unity without *any* difference, reality consists of a unity that contains *within it* internal differences. Rāmānuja explains this 'unity-with-difference' with reference to the three categories of God (Brahman, Viṣṇu, etc.) the world (*jagat*), and souls (*jīvas*). The three categories are eternally related, with the world and souls existing within, and being dependent upon the Brahman.

More specifically, Rāmānuja explains qualified non-dualism through the use of two analogies: that of body to soul, and substance to attribute or quality.

The use of the soul-body analogy to describe the relationship between God on the one hand, and the world of animate souls and inanimate matter on the other hand, is perhaps the hallmark of Rāmānuja's theology. Just as the soul of man dwells in the body and completely controls and supports it, yet remains different from the body, so God dwells in his creation (both in the world and in souls) as its support and control. The entire universe, its material reality, and its immaterial souls, are the body of God, in that He is the ruler.

Rāmānuja draws this analogy primarily from a famous section of the *Bṛhadāraṇyaka Upaniṣad* which describes the Brahman as the 'Inner Controller' (*antaryāmin*):

> 'He who, dwelling in all things, yet is other than all things, whom all things do not know, whose *body* all things are, who controls all things from within—He is your soul, the Inner Controller, the Immortal.'[12]

To adequately comprehend Rāmānuja's doctrine of the universe as the body of God, it is necessary to keep in mind his somewhat unusual definition of 'body'. He states, 'Any substance which a sentient soul is capable of completely controlling and supporting for its own purpose, and which stands to the soul in an entirely subordinate relationship, is the body of that soul.'[13] The significance of this definition is that body is not defined as physical reality, in contrast to the soul as a spiritual reality. Rather a body is simply *anything*, regardless of its form, that is under complete control of a soul. While a soul is always immaterial, a body can be either material or immaterial. Thus, what is a soul in relation to an entity which it controls can be a body in relation to an entity which controls it. This is precisely the case with the human soul (*jīva*). With respect to the physical body in which it resides, the *jīva* is a soul; but with respect to the Brahman, the *jīva* is a body, since it is controlled by Him. Thus, both the world and souls are the body of the Brahman. As such, both Difference and Identity characterize the relationship between the Brahman and the universe: Identity insofar as the Brahman dwells within and controls the universe, Difference insofar as He remains a separate being, dwelling in, but other than His body.

Rāmānuja's second method of describing the relationship of Qualified Nondualism is in terms of substance and attribute. The substance–attribute relationship expresses both Difference and

Identity in that on the one hand, they are capable of being distinguished as different realities, while on the other hand they are inseparable, in the sense that whenever one is perceived the other is perceived also. For example, a blue lily has for its substance 'lily', and its attribute 'blue'. Difference is indicated by the fact that the flower is called a 'blue lily': 'blue' in itself does not refer to the lily, nor does 'lily' necessarily refer to something blue. They refer to two different realities which are present in the object designated 'blue lily'. Identity is indicated by the fact that it is impossible to view one without the other: when looking at the flower one cannot see 'lily' without seeing 'blue', and vice versa. On the other hand, there is a difference between them in that one can distinguish between two realities that are simultaneously perceived, namely the substance of lily and the attribute of blue.

The Brahman, according to Rāmānuja, is related to the universe as substance to attribute. The world and souls are different from, yet inseparably related to God in the same manner as any attribute is related to its substance.[14]

Rāmānuja uses the soul-body relationship to describe the Brahman's relationship to the universe *after* creation, while the substance-attribute relationship applies to both before and after creation. Before creation (or creations, since there is an eternal cycle of creation and dissolution), the world and souls exist *within* the Brahman as distinct yet related realities. The world exists as unformed, undifferentiated primordial matter (*prakṛti*), while souls retain their individuality, despite being compressed to the point that name and form are not perceivable. Creation occurs when the Brahman emits the world and souls from himself and enters into them as their Inner Controller, in the manner of soul to body. Rāmānuja hence advocates *pariṇāma*, or the transformationist doctrine of creation as opposed to Śaṅkara's *vivarta* doctrine.

In any case, whether in the substance-attirbute relationship which exists before and during creation or in the body-soul relationship which exists during creation, the Brahman-universe relationship is one of unity qualified by difference.

To summarize other significant elements of Rāmānuja's thought, we could perhaps best characterize it as theistic realism.

In contrast to Śaṅkara, Rāmānuja strongly adovcates a theistic understanding of the Brahman, where he is viewed as a *personal* God rather than an impersonal absolute. In the *Śrībhāṣya*, for example,

Rāmānuja states, "The word 'Brahman' denotes the highest Person who is essentially free from all imperfections and possesses numberless classes of auspicious qualities of unsurpassable excellence."[15] Rāmānuja frequently refers to the Brahman by such theistic appelations is Īśvara, Nārāyaṇa, and Viṣṇu. For Rāmānuja, there is no higher and lower Brahman, nor two levels of truth: the personal God known through intense devotion is none other than the Brahman.

Rāmānuja's theistic interpretation of the Brahman is accompanied by a realistic interpretation of the world, where the sentient souls (*jīvas*) and insentient matter (*jagat*) are seen as being real entities, in contrast to their illusory status in the thought of Śaṅkara. According to Rāmānuja, the *jīva* is an agent; a knower; atomic in size; possessing qualities; and possessing eternal individuality. Each *jīva* is distinct from every other *jīva*, and all *jīvas* remain different from though utterly dependent on, the Brahman.

In further contrast to Śaṅkara, Rāmānuja argues that the *jīva* maintains its individuality even after release. Release essentially consists of close communion with the personal Lord rather than annihilation of the sense of individual personality. Rāmānuja argues against Śaṅkara by pointing out that loss of individuality would *deter* rather than attract seekers of the Brahman:

> If he were to realize that the effect of such activity would be loss of personal existence, he surely would turn away as soon as somebody began to tell him about release.... no sensible person exerts himself under the influence of the idea that after he himself has perished there will remain some entity termed 'pure light'![16]

With reference to the means of release, Rāmānuja points out that any discussion of salvific means presupposes a duality between seeker and object sought, knower and object to be known—a duality that Śaṅkara fails to account for. Rāmānuja identifies three *pramāṇas*: perception, inference, and Revelation, with the latter being the authoritative source of knowledge of the Brahman. Rāmānuja denies that the Brahman can be known through man's own powers without the benefit of Scripture: 'The Brahman, being raised above all contact with the senses, is not an object of perception and the other means of proof, but is to be known through Scripture only.'[17]

Rāmānuja portrays knowledge of the Brahman in terms of *bhakti*, or devotion. That is, knowledge of the Brahman is more than a mere intellectual and cognitive understanding of his true nature; rather, it is an emotional, heart-felt, constant awareness of Him. Rāmānuja often uses the word *upāsanā*, or 'steady remembrance' to characterize knowledge of God.[18] It should be added, however, that Rāmānuja also insists on the role of divine grace in man's liberation. Devotional meditation leads to release only because the Lord finds favour with the devotee and chooses to grant him liberation.[19]

NIMBĀRKA

Nimbārka, a theologian of the eleventh century, presents a theology quite similar to that of Rāmānuja, a fellow Vaiṣṇava. Nimbārka's system represents the culmination of a series of earlier Vaiṣṇava systems, all of which shared a common emphasis on the intensely emotional nature of devotion to Viṣṇu/Brahman. Nimbārka's predecessors included Hamṣa, Kumāra, and Nārada.[20] Nimārka's major work was his commentary on the *Brahma Sūtras*, the *Vedānta Pārijātasaurabha.*

In many ways Nimbārka's thought, known as *svābhāvika-bhedābheda*, closely resembles that of Rāmānuja. C. Sharma goes so far as to state—rather unfairly—that, 'it appears that he (Nimbārka) has borrowed the whole thing from his illustrious predecessor (Rāmānuja), adding his own important amendments and modifications here and there.'[21] Despite many similarities, however, Nimbārka's thought has a different tone from that of Rāmānuja's in that he bases his thought more on the Kṛṣṇa element in Vaiṣṇava thought, including its emphasis on the emotional rather than meditative nature of *bhakti.* Pereira points out that Nimbārka is the 'creator of the first Vedantic theology of Kṛṣṇa,' based largely on the *Bhāgavata Purāṇa.*[22]

The non-dualism espoused by Nimbārka is that of *bhedābheda*, or Difference (*bheda*) *and* Identity (*abheda*). While Rāmānuja describes the God-universe relationship as one of Identity qualified by Difference, with the emphasis on Identity, Nimbārka argues that Identity and Difference are *equally* true of the God-universe relationship, that both Identity and Difference are of the essence (*svābhāvika*) of the deity. Nimbārka describes the *bhedābheda* relationship in a variety of ways, but especially in terms of dependence (*pāratantṛya*) and independence (*svātantṛya*). Since the world and souls are entirely dependent on the Brahman, they are non-different from him; since God is independent and the world is dependent, they are also different. Thus, both Difference and Identity are real.[23]

Nimbārka uses several other methods to express his philosophy of *bhedābheda*. The Brahman and the universe are non-different in that the universe shares part of the Brahman's nature, while they differ in that they share *only* a part of it, lacking such qualities as omniscience and lordship.[24] Likewise, they are non-different in that the effect (universe) exists *in* the cause (Brahman), though different in that one is the effect and the other is the cause.[25] Elsewhere he states that just as all objects can be said to be permeated with substantiality, though no single one is substance itself, so all things are permeated by God while he remains different from them.[26]

A favourite metaphor of Nimbārka's for illustrating the *bhedābheda* relationship is that of the snake and its coil, a metaphor borrowed by the Nondualists from the Buddhists. While Identity is clearly indicated by the fact that the coil is nothing but the snake in a particular form, Difference is also indicated insofar as the snake is not to be identified as *only* its coiled form.

All of the above examples, Nimbārka argues, indicate that both Identity and Difference are equally true of the relationship between the Brahman and the universe.[27]

Like Rāmānuja, Nimbārka is an adherent of the *pariṇāma* doctrine of creation which acknowledges the reality of the created world as well as the Brahman's role as both efficient and material cause: 'God does not stand in need of materials to construct the world—he is all-powerful, and by his mere will he is able to create the world'.[28]

In many other areas of his thought, Nimbārka is in agreement with Rāmānuja and the other Vaiṣṇava Vedantins. The soul is a knower and agent, atomic in size, and eternally distinct from the Brahman as well as all other souls.

Liberation is attained through devotion (*bhakti*) to a personal Lord (Kṛṣṇa/Viṣṇu/Brahman). Prior to the inquiry into the nature of the Brahman, the devotee must first master the texts on duty, embodied in the precedent inquiry (*pūrva mīmāṃsā*). In liberation the soul becomes *close* to the Brahman and experiences his divine nature, but still maintains its individuality.

In all of these doctrines, Nimbārka concurs with Rāmānuja. They differ, however, in the extent to which they emphasize the emotional over the intellectual element, with Nimbārka placing much stronger emphasis on the emotional aspect of devotion and liberation.

Rāmānuja identifies *bhakti* with *upāsana* and *dhyāna*, and defines it as 'steady remembrance' or 'continuous representation' of the Lord in the devotee's mind. The emphasis is not on the emotion that the devotee feels—though emotion is present—but rather, first, on the steadiness with which one thinks about God, and secondly, the accuracy of the image itself. Thus, knowledge is a primary element of devotion.[29] In contrast, Nimbārka (like Vallabha) views *bhakti* essentially in terms of an intense emotional attachment to the Lord. Nimbārka describes *bhakti* as the state 'when by absolute self-abnegation springing from love the individual feels himself to be absolutely controlled and regulated by God and realizes himself to be a constituent of him.'[30] Elsewhere, the emotional nature of Nimbārka's thought is heard in his description of the goal of devotion:

> No goal can one perceive besides Kṛṣṇa's lotus feet, praised by gods like Brahmā and Śiva, besides Kṛṣṇa's forms, so agreeable to the fancy and so quick to reveal themselves at the devotees' desire.[31]

Finally, Nimbārka's thought places far more emphasis on the role of divine grace. Whereas Rāmānuja sees divine grace as working in conjunction with human effort, Nimbārka sees man as entirely dependent on the Lord's grace for liberation.

VALLABHA

In Vallabha we find one of the later commentators on the *Brahma Sūtras*. Born in Southern India toward the end of the fifteenth century, his main works included a commentary on the *Brahma Sūtras* (the *Aṇubhāṣya*) and a commentary on the *Bhāgavata Purāṇa* (the *Subodhinī*). In contrast to the other commentators, Vallabha drew heavily from the *Bhāgavata Purāṇa* and *Bhagavad Gītā* in developing his theology, and ranked these texts on a par with the Upaniṣad and *Brahma Sūtras*.[32]

Vallabha's philosophy is designated *Śuddhādvaita*, or Pure Non-dualism. Whereas Rāmānuja and Nimbārka recognized both Difference and Identity, Vallabha acknowledges only Indentity: everything is the Brahman. He calls his brand of non-dualism 'pure' in order to contrast it with that of Śaṅkara, who in addition to the non-dual Brahman posits *māyā*, or illusion, as a separate category. This, according to Vallabha, destroys the purity of non-dualism. In his own system, *māyā* is interpreted as the creative power of God.

Although Vallabha declares that the Brahman is all, this does not mean that the world of multiplicity is unreal. To the contrary, the world of multiplicity is entirely real in that it is the Brahman in diverse forms. The world and souls are 'parts' of the Brahman, just as sparks are parts of the fire or rays of light are parts of the sun. Thus, Vallabha is a realist monist.

Man's perception of differences between his own soul, the world, and God is explained as the result of the Brahman manifesting and concealing his three basic qualities, *sat* (being), *cit* (consciousness), and *ānanda* (joy), in different proportions. As Lord, He manifests all three qualities; as souls, He manifests *sat* and *cit* only; as the world, He manifest only *sat*.[33] Thus, there is one reality, the Brahman, who becomes many, and then suppresses certain of His qualities to produce apparent differences—namely between the world and souls—in that multiplicity.

Since the Brahman is the only reality, in truth there is no creation or dissolution of the universe. However, through His powers of manifestation (*āvirbhāva*), defined as fitness for or capacity of becoming an object of experience, and concealment (*tirobhāva*), defined as the capability of not becoming an object of experience, He creates the illusion of creation or dissolution.

Vallabha identifies the Brahman as both the material and instrumental cause of the universe. He particularly emphasizes that the Brahman creates the world directly from His own being, and that consequently the world is real, in that it is the Brahman. He contrasts this with Śaṅkara's system in which, rather than the Brahman creating a real world, the force of *māyā* somehow creates an illusory world. Vallabha acknowledges the existence of *māyā*, but interprets it as the power of the Brahman which is used to create the world.[34]

Vallabha describes the soul as being atomic in nature, 'tiny as the point of an awl.'[35] It is a small part of the Brahman, differing from Him only in that the quality of joy is suppressed in it. When the soul receives joy, like the Brahman it then becomes all-pervading. However, Vallabha emphasizes that at the same time as being all-pervading, the soul maintains its individuality. This is a very important point in his system, for as we shall see later, the goal of man is not union with the Brahman, but rather sporting with Kṛṣṇa as a separate being. The apparent inconsistency between all-pervasiveness and individuality is explained by analogy: just as sandalwood put in oil produces coolness over the entire body even though it is applied at only one spot, or just as a lamp, put in one corner of a room, illuminates the entire room, so does the soul, though an individual entity, pervade the entire universe.[36]

Concerning the path of liberation, Vallabha asserts that knowledge and action are inferior to the highest path of *bhakti*, or devotion. Thus, 'A love unshakeable and superabundant, accompanied by a knowledge of God's greatness—such is devotion. Through it alone is liberation and through no other way.'[37] Vallabha acknowledges that through knowledge one can attain omniscience, and through works in accord with *dharma* one can attain contentment of mind, but only through *bhakti* can one attain the pure love that is pleasing to God.

The goal which one aims for through the practice of *bhakti* is not union with the Brahman. Rather, one's sole desire is to please Kṛṣṇa, and this is accomplished through perfecting one's love for Him. The metaphysical union with the Brahman is shunned in favour of the union experienced by lovers, based on passionate attachment to the beloved.[38] Even an unliberated soul engaged in devotion is superior to a liberated soul that has experienced union with the Brahman. Thus,

> Those who enter into the bliss of Brahman have the experience of that bliss in their selves; but those devotees who do not enter into this state nor into the state of *jīvan-mukti*, but enjoy God with all their senses and the *antaḥkaraṇa* (heart) are better than the *jīvan-muktas*, though they may be ordinary householders.[39]

Even after a devotee gains liberation, he foregoes union in order to engage in eternal sport with Kṛṣṇa in his heaven, *Vyāpi Vaikuṇṭha*.

However, even though *bhakti* is the means by which one attains liberation, the highest form of *bhakti* is gained not through one's own efforts, but rather through the gift of God. Liberation comes only to those who have been granted grace from Kṛṣṇa. Vallabha states, 'The liberation that occurs, even in a sacred place, at some time and of some one, is only of someone furnished with Kṛṣṇa's grace, not of anyone else.'[40] While knowledge, works, and particularly devotion are all recognized as being helpful, final liberation comes only through the gift of grace.

MADHVA

Madhva stands out among his fellow commentators insofar as he presents a strictly dualist interpretation of the *Sūtras* in which God and the world are seen as eternally different from each other. However, while this separates Madhva from the other expositors, as Pereira points out, his emphasis on Difference has its roots in the oldest Vedic speculations and connects Madhva with a long tradition of Indic thinkers.[41]

Traditionally, Madhva's dates are designated as 1199 to 1278, although scholars believe that 1238 to 1317 are his actual dates.[42] Madhva relied heavily on the strongly theistic and devotional *Bhāgavata Purāṇa* in developing his theology, and the sect that he founded was the first based on that work.[43] Though a student of Śaṅkara's thought early in life, he broke away from *kevalādvaita*, and indeed all types of *advaita* to found his own system. Legends state that Madhva was an incarnation of the god Vāyu, sent to earth to destroy the heretical doctrines of Śaṅkara. Madhva claimed to refute not only the work of Śaṅkara, but also that of all twenty-one *bhāṣyas* written before him.[44] Madhva composed a total of thirty-seven works, including four commentaries of the *Sūtras*, two commentaries on the *Bhagavad Gītā*, and ten commentaries on the Upaniṣads.[45]

Madhva identifies three *prāmaṇas*, or means of knowledge, those being perception, inference, and Scripture.[46] Like the other expositors, Madhva sees Scripture as the primary source of knowledge of God. However, unlike the other major expositors who treat the Upaniṣads as the most important Scripture, Madhva adopts a far more comprehensive approach which incorportates the entire body of sacred writings, including pre-Upaniṣadic writings such as the Vedas, and post-Upaniṣadic writings such as the Purāṇas. This broader Scriptural base affords Madhva the opportunity to support his dualist interpretations of key Upaniṣadic passages that appear to assert Identity. Where an Upaniṣadic passage appears to describe Identity between the Brahman and the world, Madhva points to the many non-Upaniṣadic passages which clearly assert Difference. Since the non-Upaniṣaidc passages' meaning is clear in asserting Difference, Madhva argues that the Upaniṣadic passages which appear to assert Identity must be re-interpreted on the grounds that the truth of Scripture is consistent, and if certain passages clearly assert Difference, then other passages must be interpreted in such a way as to assert the same; otherwise, Scripture would be contradictory.

Madhva divides Scripture into authorless works such as the traditional Vedic writings, and authored works such as the epics and codes of law. Both authorless and authored Scriptures are considered to be infallible.

Given Madhva's tendency to draw from a wider range of Scripture, we see that in his commentary on the *Brahma Sūtras* he frequently identifies topical texts that differ from those acknowledged by the other major expositors. Whereas Śaṅkara and Rāmānuja, for example, identify the Upaniṣads as the source of virtually every topical text, Madhva frequently claims that topical texts come from such Scriptures as the *Ṛg Veda*, the *Gītā*, and various Purāṇas.

Madhva places strong emphasis on the role of *experience* in understanding the nature of God. He argues that experience must be valid, since otherwise we could not use Scripture, inasmuch as it is something we know through experiencing it (hearing, seeing). If experience is valid, and if experience overwhelmingly dictates a dualist perception of the world and its relationship with God, then we should accept that perception and interpret Scripture accordingly.[47] The importance that Madhva assigns to experience is beautifully expressed in his remark that, 'A hundred texts cannot make a crow white.'[48]

One of Madhva's unique contributions to Indic thought is his doctrine of the Witness, or *sākṣin*. In response to the fundamental philosophical problem of determining how we can know that that which we perceive is the truth, Madhva posits the existence of an intuitive cognitive agent which serves as our means of verifying the truth. At the level of our external senses, we are capable of making false perceptions, such as mistaking a rope for a snake. At a deeper level, however, where the Witness is operative, we have the capacity to infallibly identify what is true and what is false. Thus, there are two types of knowledge, the fallible *vṛtti-jñāna*, and the infallible *sākṣi-jñāna*.[49]

As indicated above, Madhva's theology rests on the fundamental postulate that the Brahman or God is completely and eternally different from the world of matter and souls. Madhva's primary means of describing the difference between the Brahman and His world is through the categories of independent reality (*svatantra*) and dependent reality (*paratantra*), of which there are two kinds, conscious and unconscious. While the world is utterly dependent on God for its existence, it is ontologically different from Him. Madhva sees God as the efficient cause of the world only, acting on Prime Matter (*prakṛti*), the material cause which is eternally different from Him. God acts on, but does not create *prakṛti*, which is co-eternal with Him.[50]

Madvha sees the Brahman as a personal God who creates the world and possesses an infinite number of auspicious qualities. Madhva goes to great lengths to avoid identifying God with any type of impurity. This, he believes, can only be done through a theology of pure Difference, since any type of Identity with the world would tarnish the Brahman's perfection. For this reason, Madhva rejects Rāmānuja's Qualified Non-Dualism on the grounds that if the world is the body of God, then God must experience its impurities.[51]

Madhva extends the category of Difference into five areas: God and soul; soul and soul; God and matter; matter and matter; and soul and matter. Not only does difference exist between the classes of God, soul, and matter, but within each class each member is different from every other member.

Given Madhva's total rejection of Identity, he often offers rather strained explanations of the Upaniṣadic passages which, at face value, appear to declare that the Brahman and the soul are one. At times, for instance, he argues that such passages merely affirm that the soul is *similar* to the Brahman, like the reflection of a face in the mirror is similar to the face itself. Madhva also argues that the 'Identity' declared by the Upaniṣads is like that which exists between a king and his subjects, in the sense that the latter are totally dependent on the former.[52]

Another unique aspect of Madhva's theology is his doctrine of the Specific. Since Madhva describes God as having an infinite number of attributes, the question arises as to whehter these attributes are different from or identical to Him. If they are different, then the unity of God is lost; if they are identical, then the attributes are tautologous. Madhva responds that all things possess, through the Specific, the capacity to both have attributes and yet to exist as ontologically different from those attributes, without thereby producing a disunity. Hence, as Pereira puts it, 'we have a difference that is real but does not divide'.[53]

Like the other Vaiṣṇava commentators, Madhva sees the *jīva* as eternally different from God; atomic in size, characterized as an agent; infinite in number; and dependent on the Brahman.

Like Vallabha, Madhva places strong emphasis on devotion and grace as the means to liberation. Once liberated, the individual soul enjoys all of the powers of the Lord except creation and control of the world. Madhva's view of man's final spiritual destiny differs from that of his predecessors, in that he argues that some souls are eternally damned to Hell.[54] Souls are divided into four categories: released souls such as Hiraṇyagarbha, souls which are capable of obtaining salvation, souls that are always transmigrating, and souls that are eternally damned.[55]

FOOTNOTES

1. Such a work, however, clearly is needed in the field of Vedantic studies. The works of Ghate and Radhakrishnan are at best only abbreviated efforts at completing such an analysis.

2. B.N.K. Sharma, *Brahma Sūtras*, 1:15.

3. S. Radhakrishnan, *Brahma Sūtras*, pp. 25–102.

4. Ibid., p. 28

5. Thibaut, trans., *Vedānta Sūtras with Commentary by Śaṅkara*, 1:xxv.

6. Ibid., 1:xxv.

7. Ibid., 1:61–64.

8. Ghate, *The Vedānta*, p. 22.

9. Thibaut, trans., *Vedānta Sūtras with Commentary by Śaṅkara*, 1:10.

10. Ibid., 1:14.

11. Pereira, *Hindu Theology*, p. 282.

12. *Bṛhadāraṇyaka Upaniṣad* 3:7:15.

13. Bharatan Kumarappa, *The Hindu Conception of Deity as Culminating in Rāmānuja* (London: Luzac and Co, 1934), p. 231.

14. Ibid, pp. 194–195.

15. George Thibaut, trans., *The Vedānta Sūtras of Bādarāyaṇa with the Commentary by Rāmānuja* (Delhi: Motilal Banarsidass, 1962; reprint of *Sacred Books of the East*, v. 48), p. 4.

16. Ibid, p. 70

17. Ibid, p. 161.

18. Ibid, pp. 14, 174.

19. Ibid, p. 16.

20. Das Gupta, *History of Indian Philosophy*, 3:401.

21. Chandradhar Sharma, *Indian Philosophy: A Critical Survey* (New York: Barnes and Noble, 1962), p. 363.

22. Pereira, *Hindu Theology*, p. 306.

23. Jadunath Sinha, *The Philosophy of Nimbārka* (Calcutta: Sinha Publishing House, 1973), p. 5.

24. Ibid, pp. 31–32.

25. Madan Mohan Agrawal, *The Philosophy of Nimbārka* (Gali Manihar: Shrimati Usha Agrawal, 1977), p. 29.

26. Das Gupta, *History of Indian Philosophy*, 3:431.

27. It is interesting to note that, despite the many common points shared by the theological schools of Rāmānuja and Nimbārka, members of the two schools were harsh critics of each other. See, for example, Nimbārka's critique of *Viśiṣṭādvaita* in Das Gupta, *History of Indian Philosophy*, 3:429–430.

28. Sarvepalli Radhakrishnan, *Indian Philosophy*, 2 vols., (New York: McMillan and Co., 1927), 2:754.

29. Thibaut, trans. *The Vedānta Sūtras with the Commentary by Rāmānuja*, pp. 4–5. See also J.A.B. Van Buitenen, *Rāmānuja on the Bhagavad Gītā* (Delhi: Motilal Banarsidass, 1968), pp. 108–110.

30. Das Gupta, *History of Indian Philosophy*, 4:414.

31. Pereira, *Hindu Theology*, p. 308.

32. See, for example, Mrudula Marfatia, *The Philosophy of Vallabha*, (Delhi: Munshiram Manoharlal, 1967), p. 44.

33. Das Gupta, *History of Indian Philosophy*, 4:328.

34. Ibid, p. 330.

35. Pereira, *Hindu Theology*, p. 322.

36. Marfatia, *The Philosophy of Vallabha*, pp. 20–21.

37. Pereira, *Hindu Theology*, p. 320.

38. Das Gupta, *History of Indian Philosophy*, 4:347.

39. Ibid.

40. Pereira, *Hindu Theology*, p. 322.

41. Ibid, p. 122.

42. B.N.K. Sharma, *Brahma Sūtras*, p. 101.

43. J.N. Farquhar, *An Outline of the Religious Literature of India* (Delhi: Motilal Banarsidass, 1920). p. 235.

44. Das Gupta, *History of Indian Philosophy*, 4:53.

45. B.N.K. Sharma, *The Brahma Sūtras*, 1:109–110.

46. Ibid.

47. Das Gupta, *History of Indian Philosophy*, 4:77.

48. B.N.K. Sharma, *The Brahma Sūtras*, 1:162.

49. B.N.K. Sharma, *Madhva's Teachings in His Own Words* (Bombay: Bharatiya Vidya Bhavan, 1979), pp. 46–55.

50. Das Gupta, *History of Indian Philosophy*, 4:57.

51. Raju, *Structural Depths of Indian Thought*, p. 469.

52. Ibid., pp. 469–478.

53. Pereira, *Hindu Theology*, p. 123.

54. Das Gupta, *History of Indian Philosophy*, 4:57.

55. Raju, *Structural Depths of Indian Thought*, p. 474.

CHAPTER IV

An Analysis of the *Brahma Sūtras* 1:1

The purpose of this section is to examine in detail the individual *sūtras* of the first adhyāya of the *Brahma Sūtras*, with reference to their original meaning as intended by Bādarāyaṇa. We shall identify *sūtras* according to their being grouped together into an *adhikaraṇa*; identify the topical text, with the assistance of the major expositors; translate each *sūtra*; and analyze each *sūtra* with reference to Bādarāyaṇa's apparent meaning, bearing in mind, of course, the difficulties listed above of determining Bādarāyaṇa's meaning.[1]

CATUHSŪTRĪ: INTRODUCTORY APHORISMS

The first four *sūtras* of the *Brahma Sūtras* are identitified by the expositors as being separate *adhikaraṇas*. They possess, however, a unity that fits them together as a single section, hence justifying our treatment of them as one rather than four *adhikaraṇas*.

All of the principal expositors agree on the arrangement of the first four *sūtras*, with the exception of Vallabha, who agrees with the content but alters the numbering, combining the second and third *sūtras* into one *sūtra*.[2]

The importance of these initial four *sūtras* lies in their feat of summarizing the content of the entire work: in four short sentences, Bādarāyaṇa declares the essence of what is to follow in the remaining 550 or so *sūtras*. As such, these first four *sūtras* stand as an excellent model of the concise, succinct style of *sūtra* literature.

The first *sūtra* identifies the object of the inquiry: the Brahman. The second *sūtra* defines the nature of the Brahman, namely the origin of the world. The third *sūtra* establishes the methodology for attaining such knowledge of the Brahman: the study of Scripture. Finally, the fourth *sūtra* verifies the validity of this methodology by affirming the consistency (*samanvaya*) of the Scriptural texts' declarations about the Brahman.

1.1.1: *Athāto brahmajijñāsā*

Now, then, is the inquiry into the Brahman.

Bādarāyaṇa's *Brahma Sūtras* opens with this short *sūtra* consisting of only four Sanskrit words organized into two compounds. Fortunately, it is one of the clearer *sūtras*, at least in terms of the second compound, *brahmajijñāsā*, which clearly indicates that the topic of the work which is to follow is an 'inquiry into the Brahman.' Here Bādarāyaṇa explicitly states that he is dealing with the topic of the Brahman, and not any of the several other topics that could be the subject of similar treatment, topics such as *karma, yoga,* or *sāṅkhya.*

Unfortunately, the initial compound of this *sūtra* (*athāto*) lacks such clarity and is the source of much debate betweem the expositors. *Atha*, according to Monier-Williams, is 'an auspicious and inceptive particle, not easily expressed in English'.[3] English equivalents can include 'now', 'then', and 'moreover'. *Atha* is also used as a conventional expression for opening a new topic.[4] *Atas* carries such English meanings as 'hence', 'from this', and 'therefore'. The compound, therefore, clearly conveys the general meaning that the work is about to begin an inquiry into the Brahman. The expositors, however, have taken issue with the more specific meaning that Bādarāyaṇa meant to convey by this *sūtra*.

A key point of disagreement involves the precise meaning of *atha*. Rāmānuja, for instance, argues that *atha* means 'then' in the sense that after one has first completed the study of works (*karmakāṇḍa*), one is then eligible for the study of the Brahman. Śaṅkara, in contrast, argues that the study of works is not a prerequisite for the study of the Brahman, and that *atha* means 'then' in a strictly temporal sense (i.e., the *sūtra* states simply that the study of the Brahman is now going to begin, with no reference to any requirements), or that the study of the Brahman follows after the attainment of certain spiritual qualities:

> 'the discrimination of what is eternal and what is non-eternal; the renunciation of all desire to enjoy the fruit of one's actions both here and hereafter; the acquirement of tranquility, self-restraint, and the other means, and the desire of final release.'[5]

Nimbārka, Bhāskara, and Śrīkaṇṭha agree with Rāmānuja that Bādarāyaṇa intends to state that the study of the Brahman begins only after completion of the study of works. Vallabha, on the other hand, believes that *atha* simply begins a new topic, and does not establish a prerequisite for inquiry into the Brahman.[6] Madhva tends to follow Śaṅkara's interpretation by seeing *atha* refer to the prior acquisition of certain spiritual qualities.[7]

In contrast to the disagreement over the meaning of *atha*, there is general consensus that *atas*, or 'therefore', refers to the idea that the study of and performance of works leads to only limited, finite rewards, and '*therefore*' the seeker of final release must move on to the study of the Brahman.

Our purpose, of course, is not to assess the relative merits of the expositors' various and conflicting interpretations of the *sūtras;* rather, it is to examine what Bādarāyaṇa himself has to say. What, then, can we conclude about the meaning of Bādarāyaṇa's first *sūtra*?

Unfortunately, as we will see in our examination of many of Bādarāyaṇa's *sūtras*, no clear and definitive meaning is apparent. We can only speculate from an objective point of view, in contrast to the sectarian biases of the expositors.

Given the general agreement on the meaning of *atas*, as well as the uniform acceptance in Hindu thought that the study of works leads to finite rewards while the study of the Brahman leads to release, it is reasonable to assume that this was the meaning that Bādarāyaṇa meant to convey through *atas*. With regard to *atha*, however, no such firm conclusion can be drawn. The fact that, later in the *Brahma Sūtras*, Bādarāyaṇa makes reference to Jaimini as an authority, suggests that he was familiar with and respected the works tradition.[8] It does not necessarily follow, however, that Bādarāyaṇa therefore held that the study of works was a necessary prerequisite to the study of the Brahman. Indeed, one can argue that if Bādarāyaṇa indeed had held such a position, he most likely would have *stated* this position somehwere in his work, yet no such declaration is found in the *Brahma Sūtras*. On the other hand, if we accept the traditional view that the *Brahma Sūtras* and Jaimini's *Mīmāṃsā Sūtras* are part of one *Mīmāṃsā* (*Pūrva* and *Uttara*), then it could be deduced that the prerequisite nature of works was a given, and hence not something which Bādarāyaṇa needed to declare. Perhaps the only conclusive interpretation of the first *sūtra* is that it announces the initiation of the inquiry of the Brahman: whether or not Bādarāyaṇa believed that this inquiry had to be preceded by an inquiry into works must be left unanswered.

Before moving on to the next *sūtra*, a final point should be made regarding this first verse. In our attempt to discern the original. meaning of the *Brahma Sūtras*, we will be employing at least three methodologies. First, we will be attempting to identify Bādarāyaṇa's intent through an unbiased and objective translation of each *sūtra*. Secondly, we will at times use the topical texts, alleged to be those intended to be called to mind by Bādarāyaṇa (*viṣaya vākya*) to infer Bādarāyaṇa's probable meaning. In other words, if there is general agreement on the topical text to which a *sūtra* refers, we can infer that Bādarāyaṇa concurred with the theology expresssed in that topical text (bearing in mind, of course, that the theology of some of the topical texts is unclear). Thirdly, we will attempt to identify Bādarāyaṇa's theology through judicious inferences based on his own *sūtras*: inferences based on the ordering of *sūtras*, the relationship between *sūtras*, word selection within *sūtras*, and other factors which seem to *suggest* something beyond that which Bādarāyaṇa clearly *states*.

Such an inferential deduction can be made on the *sūtra* we have just examined. In particular, one can infer that by declaring the Brahman to be an object of inquiry, Bādarāyaṇa is thereby acknowledging some type of *difference* (*bheda*) between the Brahman and the world, since only if there is an inquirer distinct from the object of his inquiry, does the concept of inquiry make sense. The specific nature of this difference between the Brahman and the world cannot be inferred from this *sūtra*, leaving room for Rāmānuja, Nimbārka, Madhva, and the rest to insert their own sectarian intepretations. That *some* type of difference is implied is, however, difficult to deny. This inference is made quite strongly in the commentaries of Rāmānuja, Madhva, and lesser known expositor, Vedānta Deśika.[9] Śaṅkara attempts to deny this point through his rather clever doctrine of the two levels of truth, but nowhere in the *Brahma Sūtras* is such a doctrine found,[10] leading us to concur with the dualists (whether pure or qualified) that Bādarāyaṇa believes that some type of difference exists between the Brahman and the world.

1.1.2: *Janmādyasya yataḥ*

The Brahman is that from which comes the origin, preservation, and destruction of this world.

Bādarāyaṇa's second *sūtra* provides us with an excellent illustration of some of the difficulties encountered in translating the *Brahma*

Sūtras. Literally, the *sūtra* reads, 'From which the origin, etc., of this.' Note, first of all, that the *sūtra* does not include a subject: *what* is the origin, etc., of this? Secondly, to what 'this' does the word *yasya* ('of this') refer? Finally, what does *ādi* ('etc.') refer to in the compound, *janmādi?* Without this information the *sūtra* makes little or no sense, yet it is typical of the *sūtra* style to leave out such crucial information. Such information was, of course, assumed to be known by the student, thereby making sense of the *sūtra*.

In the case of this particular *sūtra*, there is universal agreement among the expositors regarding the content of these 'missing pieces.' The subject, carried over from the previous *sūtra*, is the Brahman; 'of this' refers to 'of this world'; and 'etc.' refers to the preservation and dissolution of the world, which along with its creation (*janma*) form the traditional threefold cyclical scheme which characterizes God's relationship to the world. Hence, the *sūtra* serves as a definition of the Brahman, defining it as the source of the creation, preservation, and dissolution of the world. Only Madhva offers a slightly different interpretation, in that he defines '*ādi*' as referring to eight, rather than three, categories: creation (*sṛṣṭi*), preservation (*sthiti*), destruction (*saṃhāra*), control (*niyama*), knowledge (*jñāna*), ignorance (*ajñāna*), bondage (*bandha*), and release (mokṣa).[11]

In terms of our attempt to discover the original meaning of the *Brahma Sūtras*, this *sūtra* is an important one. Having announced in the first *sūtra* that the topic is the Brahman, in the second *sūtra* Bādarāyaṇa proceeds to offer a definition or description of the Brahman. Since this is the first such description offered by Bādaryāṇa, it is logical to assume that he considered it to be an *essential* definition of it: it would hardly make sense, for instance, to present a secondary, unimportant definition of the Brahman at such an early point in the work (although Śaṅkara tends to advocate this very position, arguing that the Brahman's creatorship is an accidental quality (*taṭastha lakṣaṇa*).[12] Since this *sūtra* defines the Brahman in terms of being the creator (as well as preserver and destroyer) of the world, we can therefore assume that Bādarāyaṇa understood the Brahman primarily, or at least significantly, in terms of its role as creator. This conclusion will be further validated later on, as we see several *sūtras* in which Bādarāyaṇa refers to the Brahman as the creator of the world.

Sūtra 1.1.2 also enables us to confirm the point that we made with reference to the theological implications of *sūtra* 1.1.1, namely that

Bādarāyaṇa perceives God as in some manner *different* from the world. In the first *sūtra*, we noticed that by declaring the need for an inquiry into the Brahman, Bādarāyaṇa implies the existence of some type of difference between the Brahman, the object of the inquiry, and man, the subject of the inquiry. Through a similar process of theological deduction, we can assert that in 1.1.2, by describing the Brahman as creator of the world, Bādarāyaṇa must believe in *some* type of difference between the Brahman the creator and the world which is his creation. While we cannot agree with Madhva that this *sūtra* confirms that Bādarāyaṇa was a strict dualist,[13] it is difficult to deny that *some* type of dualism lies behind Bādarāyaṇa's definition of the Brahman as creator of the world. As to the specific type of dualism which Bādarāyaṇa advocated (for example, Rāmānuja's Qualified Non-dualism), we cannot offer an answer, at least not on the basis of this *sūtra*.

Śaṅkara, of course, argues that the creation of the world is true in only a relative sense, at the lower level of truth, and that at the higher level of truth there is only the one undifferentiated reality which is the Brahman. While Śaṅkara may describe this position with considerable eloquence and defend it with some impressive theologizing, he offers no evidence to demonstrate that this is also Bādarāyaṇa's position. Bādarāyaṇa, in fact, makes no mention of two levels of truth: therefore, it is logical to assume that the statements made by him are made in a straight forward, clear-cut manner. If Bādarāyaṇa states that the Brahman is the creator of the world, we must assume that he means just that, since he provides no reason for assuming that he means something different from what he actually says.

Part of our approach in analysing the *Braham Sūtras* is to look at not only the meaning of each *individual sūtra*, but also the meaning that can be deduced by looking at the structuring of the *sūtras*. This latter approach can be useful in looking at the first two *sūtras*, for when we look at them together, we are led to an even stronger sense of Bādarāyaṇa's belief in some type of difference between the Brahman and the world. We say this because, first of all, two *consecutive sūtras* imply some type of difference, and secondly, because the very *first two sūtras* of the entire work affirm difference. Surely if the element of difference was rejected or even considered of secondary importance by Bādarāyaṇa, he would not have begun his work with two *sūtras* that so strongly affirm difference.

Finally, *sūtra* 1.1.2 can be seen as suggesting that Bādarāyaṇa is not only a dualist of sorts but also a *realist* of sorts. He affirms that the Brahman creates (and preserves and destroys) the world. In the absence of any statement to the contrary, either here or anywhere else in the *Brahma Sūtras*, we can conclude that Bādarāyaṇa believes that the Brahman creates a real world. Śaṅkara's position that creation is an illusion perceived by those who lack clear knowledge is simply not found anywhere in Bādarāyaṇa's work.

1.1.3: *Śāstrayonitvāt*

Scripture is the source of the knowledge of the Brahman.

Having declared the object of his inquiry (the Brahman) in 1.1.1, and having defined the Brahman in 1.1.2, Bādarāyaṇa now proceeds to identify the source from which (*yonitvāt*) we derive knowledge of the Brahman: Scripture.

This *sūtra*, like the previous *sūtra*, offers some ambiguity for the translator due to its deletion of key words. Translated literally, the *sūtra* seems to mean 'from the source (*yonitvāt*) which is Scripture (*Śāstra*).' There is no indication within the *sūtra* itself that the knowledge of the Brahman is that which is derived from the source which is Scripture; rather, this is an element that we must add through logical inference from the two previous *sūtras*.

This ambiguity has led some of the expositors to offer two interpretations of 1.1.3. Śaṅkara, for instance, in addition to the interpretation we have just given, also suggests that the *sūtra* could mean 'the Brahman is the source of Scripture,' a rather surprising assertion considering that it contradicts the traditional Vedic view that Scripture is impersonally originent (*apauruṣeya*) or the Brahman in the form of sound.[14] There is also some logic in arguing that just as 1.1.2 declared one of the Brahman's great attributes, that of world creation, so also 1.1.3 declares another of its great attributes, that of creating Scripture.

Madhva, however, offers what seems to be a reasonable objection to this interpretation, declaring that since 1.1.2 has already declared that the Brahman is the creator of the world, to state in 1.1.3 that it is the creator of Scripture is redundant, since 1.1.2 implies that it is the creator of everything, Scripture presumably included.[15]

As a further argument against Śaṅkara's second interpretation of the third *sūtra*, it should be noted that when the first interpretation is accepted (i.e., knowledge of the Brahman comes from Scripture), there is a logical flow that emerges through the first three *sūtras:* identification of the topic (the Brahman), definition of the topic (the Brahman is creator of the world), and identification of the source of knowledge of the topic (Scripture).

Yet another case for this interpretation of the third *sūtra* is made by Rāmānuja, who does so, however, only by positing a *pūrvapakṣa* to *sūtra* 1.1.2—something which, of course, is Rāmānuja's own device and not part of Bādarāyaṇa's work. According to Rāmānuja, the *pūrvapakṣin* responds to 1.1.2 by arguing that if the Brahman's status as creator can be known through reasoning—said reasoning having been given by Rāmānuja to support the validity of 1.1.2—then the Brahman can be known without the benefit of Scripture. Rāmānuja sees 1.1.3 as a response to this argument, countering it with an affirmation that Scripture (and Scripture *alone*) is the source of the knowledge of the Brahman.[16] Given these arguments in favour of interpreting 1.1.3 as declaring Scripture to be the source of the Brahman knowledge, it is this interpretation which we will accept.

It is unfortunate, however, that Bādarāyaṇa, does not clarify his own position on the relationship between reason and revelation: he declares that the Brahman is known through Scripture, but fails to address the roles played by reason and experience. It should be noted that the doctrine that knowledge of God comes only through revealed Scripture is a very ancient Hindu doctrine, traceable back to the Vedic concept of the eternal nature of sound, and the consequent eternal status of Scripture. Hinduism thus reveals itself to be a 'religion of the Word' in much the same way as Christianity, Judaism, and Islam. Unfortunately, uncritical Westerners have often overlooked this aspect of Hinduism, leading to the completely unfounded contrast between 'mystical' India, and the 'Scriptural' or 'rational' West. In reality, Hinduism values Scripture as highly as any Western religion does.

One final point must be mentioned regarding *sūtra* 1.1.3, with reference to what we can infer from it about Bādarāyaṇa's theology. If the Brahman is known through Scripture, which is revealed to man from a transcendent source, does this not imply that the Brahman must be in some sense *different* from the world? If the Brahman were identical to the world, then it could be known by experiencing or learning about the world. This *sūtra* states something different: the Brahman is known through *Scripture*, and therefore we can infer that Bādarāyaṇa assumes that the Brahman in some way is different from the world. Our confidence in making such an inference is based on the previous two *sūtras*, both of which, as we have seen above, also seem to infer difference. Thus, with the *Brahma Sūtras* beginning with three consecutive *sūtras* that can quite easily be interpreted as asserting some type of difference between the Brahman and the world, we are led to conclude that Bādarāyaṇa's original intent was to advocate for some type of *bheda* theology.

1.1.4: *Tattu samanvayāt*

But that (i.e., Scripture's authority) is shown from the connected meaning of the texts.

Having established in the third *sūtra* that Scripture is the source of knowledge of the Brahman, in 1.1.4 Bādarāyaṇa next defends the claim that Scripture holds such a position on the grounds that all Scripture declares the same, consistent truths about the Brahman. If, of course, Scripture made contradictory assertions about the Brahman, this would call into question its validity as an authoritative source. Here Bādarāyaṇa affirms the validity of Scripture by asserting its consistency.

Typically, of course, the *sūtra*'s words leave room for and indeed demand, that the interpreter read beyond the three words of the *sūtra* to arrive at an understandable interpretation. In the first compound, for instance (*tat-tu*), both words lack clear reference. 'But' (*tu*) obviously responds to an objection or counter-argument, but Bādarāyaṇa does not indicate what that position might be. It would seem reasonable, however, to follow Radhakrishnan in accepting the majority position of the expositors that 'but' counters the argument that Scripture presents many different and often conflicting descriptions of the Brahman, and therefore cannot act as a valid source for knowledge of the Brahman.[17]

Similarly, 'that' (*tat*) contains no referent within the *sūtra* itself, but again it seems reasonable to conclude that the referent is the assertion made in the previous *sūtra* (1.1.3), namely that the Brahman is known through Scripture.

In a sense, 1.1.4 functions as the justification for the entire *Brahma Sūtras*: the fourth *sūtra* asserts that Scripture presents a consistent and unitary truth about the Brahman, and the remainder of the work serves as an attempt to prove that this is true. The *Brahma Sūtras* attempt to demonstrate that behind the many different and, at times, seemingly contradictory statements about the Brahman, there is a unifying concordance (*samanvaya*) which makes all the apparent discrepancies disappear.

As an aside, it is interesting to note specifically *how* the expositors see Bādarāyaṇa as organizing his defense of Scripture's *samānvaya.* Śaṅkara, for instance, argues that *pāda* one deals with passages that appear to clearly refer to the Brahman; *pādas* two and three refer to indefinite references to the Brahman, with *pāda* two dealing with the qualified Brahman and *pāda* three dealing with the pure Brahman; and *pāda* four addresses passages that appear to refer to *pradhāna* (primordial matter). This, however, is a rather dubious explanation of Bādarāyaṇa's scheme since Bādarāyaṇa himself makes no reference to the two aspects of the Brahman that are such an essential part of Śaṅkara's system.

A much more convincing explanation of the structure through which Bādarāyaṇa defends Scripture's authority is presented by Madhva. According to Madhva, each chapter (*adhyāya*) examines words or phrases in Scripture that fall under three categories:

1. *Anyatraprasiddha* (The Brahman's equivalent names)—words which commonly refer to something other than the Brahman, but which could refer to the Brahman through their secondary meaning.
2. *Ubhayatraprasiddha* (The Brahman's ambivalent names)—words which could equally refer to the Brahman or to something other than the Brahman.
3. *Anyatraivaprasiddha* (The Brahman's alterivalent names)—words which are commonly understood to refer *solely* to something other than the Brahman.

Finally, each of these classes is divided into two categories: *nāmātmakaśabda*, or proper name and non-significant terms, and *liṅgātmaka*, or descriptive and significant terms.[18]

TOPIC FIVE: INTELLIGIBILITY

1.1.5: *Īkṣaternāśabdam*

Version A: The scripturally unwarranted Prime Matter (*Pradhāna*) is not the source of the world because of the reference to 'thinking' (in the Scriptural passage which describes this source: "This being was *thinking* to itself, 'Would that I were many'." *Chāndogya Upaniṣad* 6:2:3:).

Version B: The Brahman is not inexpressible, because it is an object of knowledge (as Scripture declares: 'The word that all the Vedas reveal, that all penances proclaim, and in yearning for which men live as celibate students—I shall tell you this word briefly: t is OM.' *Kaṭha Upaniṣad* 1:2:15).

1.1.6: *Gauṇaścennātmaśabdāt*

Version A: Can it be said that the term 'thinking' here has a figurative sense and can thus be applied to the unconscious Prime Matter?

No, because Scripture uses the word 'Self', which is conscious and to whom 'thinking' can be applied, (as seen in the passage, "That subtle essence is the inbeing of all this existence. It is Reality. It is the Self. You are it, 'Svetaketu',"). *Chāndogya Upaniṣad* 6:4:13.

Version B: Can it be that the individual soul is referred to as the object of knowledge?

No, because in referring to it, Scripture uses the word, 'Self', which designates the Supreme Self, not the individual soul (same topical text).

1.1.7: *Tanniṣṭhasya mokṣopadeśāt*

Version A: The Being (*Sat*) that Scripture says creates the world is the Brahman, because Scripture declares that release comes only from that Being (as in the passage, 'I shall remain here only as long as I shall not be released. Then I shall reach perfection.' *Chāndogya Upaniṣad* 6:14:2); and it is known that release never comes from Prime Matter.

Version B: The Being that Scripture says creates the world must be the Brahman, because Scripture also teaches that release comes to him who is devoted to that Being, and it is known that release never comes from devotion to the individual soul (as in the passage, 'When a man really perceives the Self, that God, the Lord of what was and what will be, he is not revulsed.' *Bṛhadāraṇyaka Upaniṣad* 4:4:15).

1.1.8: *Heyatvāvacanāc ca*

Version A: Furthermore, there is no declaration that the Being should be rejected, a declaration that would be necessary if the Being referred to Prime Matter, for Matter is to be transcended if liberation is to be attained, according to the Sāṅkhya teaching itself.

Verson B: Furthermore, there is no declaration that the Being should be rejected, a declaration that would be necessary if the Being referred to the individual soul. (In Scripture's words, 'In Him the heavens, the earth and the sky are woven, and the mind with all the Breaths. Know Him alone to be the unique Self, renounce all other words! He is the bridge of immortality.' *Muṇḍaka Upaniṣad* 2:2:5).

1.1.9: *Svāpyayāt*

Version A: Because the topical text declares that a sleeping man becomes united with Being and enters his Self, Prime Matter cannot be that Being, since the intelligent Self would never enter the non-intelligent Prime Matter. (As Scripture maintains, 'When a man sleeps, my dear boy, he unites with the Real, he goes to his own' *Chāndogya Upaniṣad* 6:4:13).

Version B: Because the topical text declares that a sleeping man becomes united with Being and enters his Self, that Being must refer to the Brahman, not the individual soul.

1.1.10: *Gatisāmānyāt*

Versions A and B: The teachings are uniform in this regard.

1.1.11: *Śrutatvācca*

Verions A and B: And so Revelation proclaims the Brahman (in words such as the following: 'That is fullness, this is fullness; fullness proceeds from fullness. when one takes fullness out of fullness, fullness, remains.' *Bṛihadāraṇyaka Upaniṣad* 5:1:1).

The first extended topic of the *Brahma Sūtras* runs a total of seven verses, from *sūtra* 1.1.5 to 1.1.11. It is an interesting and challenging topic, in that there are at least two rather convincing interpretations of the topic, one offered by Rāmānuja, Śaṅkara, and Nimbārka (designated here as Version A), the other offered by Madhva (designated as Version B).

According to version A, the purpose of this topic is to refute the doctrine that *Pradhāna*, or Prime Matter, is the source of the creation of the world, and hence, as the result of *sūtra* 1.1.2, is the topic of the *Brahma Sūtras*. The doctrine of Prime Matter comes from the

Sāṅkhya theological school, which believes in a dualist system in which there is eternal difference between unconscious Prime Matter and conscious Spirit (*Puruṣa*).[19]

According to Rāmānuja, Śaṅkara, and Nimbārka, the topical text (*viṣaya-vākya*) for this topic comes from the *Chāndogya Upaniṣad*, 6:2:3:

> This Being (*sat*) thought to itself: 'Would that I were many. Let me procreate myself.'

In response to the Sāṅkhya argument that this verse declares that creation is done by *sat*, which is impersonal being and hence equivalent to the Sāṅkhya category of Prime Matter, Bādarāyaṇa (according to the version A) declares that Prime Matter cannot be referred to by *sat*, since the verse refers to *sat* as engaging in the process of 'thinking' (*ikṣater*), a process that the unconscious Prime Matter cannot engage in.

The remaining *sūtras* of this topic further support the position that the Brahman, not Prime Matter, is the Being referred to as creating the world in the topical text. *Sūtra* 1.1.6 counters the argument that 'thinking' is used in only a figurative sense, on the grounds that the presence of word 'Self' makes a figurative interpretation unnecessary. *Sūtra* 1.1.7 points out that this Being is also described as the object of devotion and source of release, a description that could only be made of the Brahman, and never of Prime Matter which even the Sāṅkhyas acknowledge as not producing liberation. Several interpretations of 1.1.8 are possible, not all of which need to be addressed here. In essence, the *sūtra* states that if the Being is identified with Prime Matter, then other statements made in the topical text would have to be declared invalid. Since such statements are *not* declared invalid, then it can be assumed that the text never assumes that the Being is Prime Matter.[20] In 1.1.9, Bādarāyaṇa refers to the statement that a sleeping man enters this Being, which therefore cannot be Prime Matter since an intelligent soul would never enter unintelligent matter. Finally, the topic closes with *sūtra* 1.1.10 declaring that all teachers agree that the Brahman, not Prime Matter, creates the world, and 1.1.11 declaring that Scripture directly states so. This practice of ending an extended topic by referring to the agreement of all Scripture on the issue being examined is a tactic employed by Bādarāyaṇa at several places in the *Brahma Sūtras*, a tactic that clinches his position by seemingly declaring, 'Enough arguing!

Scripture declares what is true, and this is what we accept.'

Whereas Rāmānuja, Śaṅkara, and Nimbārka see this topic as arguing against the doctrine that Prime Matter is the source of creation, Madhva takes a radically different approach, interpreting the topic as an affirmation that the Brahman is a knowable Being, characterized by an infinite number of supreme qualities that can be perceived by his devotees.

While Śaṅkara, Rāmānuja, and Nimbārka choose *Chāndogya* 6:2:3 as the topical text, Madhva identifies different five topical texts:

(1) 'He (the seeker) perceives the Supreme One through initiation by the exalted Brahman' (*Praśna Upaniṣad*, v. 5).
(2) 'He should perceive the Supreme in his own self' (*Bṛhadāraṇyaka Upaniṣad*, 4:4:23).
(3) 'Receiving clear ideas from Scripture, he shall endeavour to obtain direct vision' (*Bṛhadāraṇyaka Upaniṣad*, 4:4:21).
(4) 'All the Revelations speak primarily of Him' (*Kaṭha Upaniṣad*, 1:2:15).
(5) 'The One chiefly denoted by words of Scripture' (*Rig Veda*, 1:164:46).[21]

Hence, Madhva interprets *sūtra* 1.1.5 as an assertion that the Brahman is not inexpressible, or beyond the realm of words, since Scripture itself declares that he is knowable. The remaining *sūtras* of this topic counter the objection that the topical text describes the *individual* soul (*jīva*), not the Supreme Self (*Ātman*) or the Brahman, as capable of being known. In 1.1.6, this point is made by indicating that the word *Ātman* is actually present in the topical text, thereby eliminating any grounds for assuming that the individual soul is the subject. In 1.1.7 Bādarāyaṇa argues that since the texts declare that release is granted to those who seek this Self, surely it must be the Brahman and not the individual soul. *Sūtra* 1.1.8 adds that since there is no statement that this being should be rejected, by implication it therefore must be the Brahman. The ninth *sūtra* points out that since the topical texts declare that the soul enters this self, surely it must be the Brahman. Finally, *sūtra* ten proclaims that all teachings agree on this point, and *sūtra* eleven adds that revelation declares it to be true.

This first extended topic of the *Brahma Sūtras* serves as an excellent example of how easily different interpretations can be derived from the very same *sūtras*. Madhva on the one hand, and

Śaṅkara, Rāmānuja, and Nimbārka on the other hand provide us with quite different interpretations, both of which appear to be reasonably derived from Bādarāyaṇa's *sūtras*. Indeed, there is even at least one more interpretation which we have not mentioned, that being the one of Baladeva, who sees this topic as addressing the issue of the qualified (*saguṇa*) and unqualified (*nirguṇa*) Brahman, with Baladeva interpreting Bādarāyaṇa's *sūtras* as speaking in favour of the unqualified Brahman.[22] This, of course, is the exact opposite of Madhva's interpretation, who sees the section as declaring that the Brahman does have qualities, and therefore is knowable and expressible.

The important role played by the topical text (*viṣaya-vākya*) also is demonstrated in this section. The section consists of an initial theological position, followed by six *sūtras* that support that position by reference to the topical text. The entire line of thought is based on specific words found in the topical text, yet Bādarāyaṇa does not supply us with that text: instead we must rely on the judgments of the expositors, who among themselves disagree on the topical text. If, for example, one accepts the topical text of Rāmānuja, his rendering of the *sūtras* appears to be sound; if, on the other hand, one starts with Madhva's topical texts, then his interpretation of the *sūtras* is equally convincing.

How, then, are we to arrive at a definitive interpretation of what Bādarāyaṇa meant in this section? Unfortunately, as in many sections of the *Brahma Sūtras*, the answer is that we *cannot* arrive at a definitive, absolutely certain interpretation. Rather, we must be content to seek what appears to be the most reasonable among several possible interpretations. In doing so, our methodology must shift from a focus on individual *sūtras* to a look at the larger structure and content of the *Brahma Sūtras*.

From this broader perspective, Baladeva's interpretation immediately becomes suspect: why should we assume that the subject of the section is the *nirguṇa* Brahman when *nowhere in his entire work* does Bādarāyaṇa directly refer to the *nirguṇa* Brahman in a *sūtra*. If not a single *sūtra* explicitly refers to the *nirguṇa* Brahman, is it likely that an entire section refers to it, and, indeed, declares it to be superior to the qualified Brahman?

The position of Rāmānuja, Śaṅkara, and Nimbārka which interprets the *sūtras* as arguing against the Sāṅkhya doctrine of creation from Prime Matter also becomes suspect when the broader structure of the *Brahma Sūtras* is considered. If the *Brahma Sūtras* is indeed a *systematic* treatment of the Vedantic texts, then it would be reasonable to assume an *orderliness* in the manner in which the work addresses the various issues that arise from the texts. Likewise, one would presume to find a logical connection between the various topical sections. The interpretation of Śaṅkara, etc., is somewhat lacking in both of these areas. Why, for instance, does Bādarāyaṇa address the Sāṅkhya doctrine of Prime Matter at this point in his work, when he does the same thing again later in the work (in the last section of Chapter 1)? A systematic work by definition should address a given topic as a unity, not scattered in different places.

But the interpretation of Śaṅkara, etc., also is suspect on the grounds that there is only a rather weak connection between *sūtra* 1.1.4 and the subsequent topical sections, 1.1.5 to 1.1.11, and likewise, the topics following 1.1.5 to 1.1.11 do not seem to follow from it. While 1.1.5 to 1.1.11 deals with creation by affirming that Prime Matter is not the source of creation, the following topics affirm that various texts refer to the Brahman, with no reference to Prime Matter, just as there was no reference to it in the first four *sūtras*. Of course, one can argue that the topic must begin somewhere, but would it not be more logical to insert it at only one point, and at a point that is consistent with the focus of the surrounding *sūtras*?

In contrast, Madhva's interpretation of the first section fits nicely with the preceding and subsequent *sūtras*, and hence lends a stronger sense of logic and order to the work. First, Madhva's interpretation carries over the same subject (the Brahman) from the previous *sūtra*, rather than inserting the subject of Prime Matter on no apparent grounds. Secondly, Madhva's interpretation fits nicely with the preceding *sūtras*: since 1.1.3 and 1.1.4 had declared that the Brahman is known through the uniform truth of Scriptural texts, 1.1.5 to 1.1.11 counters the logical objection that the Brahman is not capable of being described and hence known through the study of Scripture. Finally, Madhva's interpretation fits well with the following *sūtras*, in that while 1.1.5–11 declares that the Brahman can be described, the subsequent topics offer the various descriptions of Him found in Scripture.

To conclude our analysis of this section, we can say that while an analysis of the section by itself can yield several equally tenable interpretations, when looked at in the broader context of the entire work as a *systematic* treatise, Madhva's interpretation appears to be far more convincing.[23]

It should also be noted that, with reference to our attempt to identify Bādarāyaṇa's own theological position, this section provides strong evidence that Bādarāyaṇa perceived the Brahman as a qualified (*saguṇa*) being, rather than the qualityless, undifferentiated One of pure non-dualism.

TOPIC 6: THE SELF CONSISTING OF JOY

1.1.12: *Ānandamayo'bhyāsāt*

The Brahman is the Joyful, becasue Revelation, when referring to Him, repeatedly uses the word 'joy'. (Scripture begins with the words: 'Now this is an inquiry into joy.' Then, describing the degrees of the intensity of joy, from the human to the divine, using the word 'joy' over twenty times, the passage concludes: 'A man who knows this, when he departs from the world, passes over to the Self who is the fullness of food, the Self who is the fullness of breath, the Self who is the fullness of mind, the Self who is the fullness of knowledge, the Self who is the fullness of Joy.' *Taittirīya Upaniṣad* 2:8:1).

1.1.13: *Vikāraśabdānneti cenna prācuryāt*

Is it not true that the suffix '-ful' (*maya*) only signifies 'having' joy or being 'made of' joy, and so cannot refer to the Brahman?

No, because '-ful' here signifies 'fullness' of joy, and hence denotes the Brahman.

1.1.14: *Tadhetu vyapadeśāca*

And becasue the Brahman is designated elsewhere as the cause of joy, therefore he must be full of joy (Scripture declares: 'He is truly Savor itself. One who relishes this Savor is filled with joy. If this pervasive Being were not joy, who could exhale, who could inhale? He alone is the cause of Joy.' *Taittirīya Upaniṣad* 2:7).

1.1.15: *Māntravarṇikam eva ca gīyate*

The 'Joy' Scripture (*Taittirīya Upaniṣad*) celebrates the Brahman as joyful in both its hymnic and ritual portions.

1.1.16: *Netaro'nupaptteḥ*

The fullness of joy does not refer to the other self, the individual soul, because it is unfit to be that.

1.1.17: *Bhedavyapadeśācca*

And because the individual soul and the Self are declared to be different (one being the fearless and the other prone to fear, in Scriptural passages like, 'When he finds fearlessness and security in that invisible, impersonal, ineffable and independent Being, then he will have attained fearlessness. But if he makes the slightest dent within it, he will have cause to fear.' *Taittirīya Upaniṣad* 2:7).

1.1.18: *Kāmācca nānumānapekṣā*

Creation (which ensues from this fullness of joy) cannot be inferred (as the unconscious Matter of the Sāṅkhya can), since creation springs from His will (as Scripture attests: "He willed, 'Let me be many, let me generate.' Then He kindled with heat. Being kindled, He emitted everything, whatever exists." *Taittirīya Upaniṣad* 2:6).

1.1.19: *Asminnasya ca tadyogam śāsti*

Revelation also teaches the union of the individual soul with that which is the fullness of joy, or the Brahman (in Scripture's words: 'The Brahman is reality, knowledge, infinity. He who knows it to be hidden in the abyss of the heart, in the highest heaven, he relishes all joys along with the wise Brahman.' *Taittirīya Upaniṣad* 2:1).

There is general agreement among the expositors that the topical text for this section is the *Taittirīya Upaniṣad* 2:5:

> Verily, other than and within that one that consists of understanding is a self that is the fullness of joy. By that this is filled. That one, indeed, has the form of a person.

This verse is preceded by a series of verses which define a series of selves (consisting respectively of food, breath, mind, understanding, and, finally, joy), each apparently higher than the other.

According to Rāmānuja and Śaṅkara, this topic begins an extended section consisting of several topics which examine those words whose meaning does not clearly refer to the Brahman. In contrast, Madhva sees this section as beginning an extended section which describes the Brahman's many wonderful qualities.

The basic thesis of this section is declared in 1.1.12, namely that the Self consisting of joy (*ānandamayo*) is the Highest Self, or the Brahman. The gounds for making this statement are that Scripture repeatedly (*abhyāsāt*) declares this to be so. This is a ground for proof that is used quite frequently by Bādarāyaṇa and is indicative of the high esteem in which he holds the authority of Scripture. Indeed, Bādarāyaṇa defends his position more often by appeal to Scritpure than by appeal to reason.[24]

This first verse of the section presents a typical problem for the interpreter of the *Brahma Sūtras*: the absence of a written subject. The two words of the *sūtra* are quite clear (*ānandamayo*—consisting of joy; and *abhyāsāt*—because of repetition), but the *sūtra* itself makes no reference to what is referred to by these words. This, of course, becomes apparent by referring to the topical text, but then again, the topical text is not given by Bādarāyaṇa, but rather must be inferred from another source. Fortunately, there is agreement among the expositors regarding the topical text for this particular *sūtra*, but the potential for conflict that is created by the fact that Bādarāyaṇa does not list the topical text is quite obvious.

Finally, with reference to 1.1.12, it should be noted that this is a clear affirmation that Bādarāyaṇa perceives the Brahman as possessing qualities, a point which we also saw demonstrated in the previous topical section.

In 1.1.13, Bādarāyaṇa counters an objection: how can '*ānandamaya*' refer to the Brahman, since the suffix '*-maya*' denotes 'being made from', and the Brahman, as creator of the universe (see 1.1.2) is not made from anything, but rather is eternally existent. Bādarāyaṇa responds that in this case, the suffix '*-maya*' has the meaning of 'containing an abundance of', and hence the Brahman is described as having an abundance of, rather than being made from, joy.

In 1.1.14, Bādarāyaṇa again supports his position by appealing to Scripture, this time pointing out that since Scripture also declares that the Brahman creates joy, surely he must abound in it.

A further challenge arises in the form of an assertion that the Brahman is not clearly designated as the topic of the Upaniṣadic passages in question. Bādarāyaṇa responds that the Brahman is clearly the topic of the *mantra* sung at the beginning of the chapter, and since no other topic is introduced, it must be assumed that he remains the topic until otherwise stated. This is a method of proof that we shall see Bādarāyaṇa employ at other points in the *Brahma Sūtras.*

Sūtra 1.1.16 begins a very important section, extending through *sūtra* 1.1.19, in which Bādarāyaṇa clearly declares that there is difference between the Brahman and the individual soul.[25] In 1.1.16, Bādarāyaṇa states that the Joyful Self must be the Highest Self and no other (*na itaraḥ*) since qualities ascribed to it are not applicable (*anupapatti*) to the individual self. The specific quality that Bādarāyaṇa refers to is that of creatorship, which is ascribed to the Joyful Self in *Taittirīya Upaniṣad* 2:6: "He desired: 'Would that I were many! Let me procreate myself...' As the real, he became whatever there is here." This is significant in that the recurrence of the doctrine of the Brahman as creator, asserted earlier at a key point in 1.1.2, again suggests that Bādarāyaṇa viewed creatorship as an essential quality of the Brahman, and indeed perhaps his most fundamental quality. If, as we argued earlier, belief in a creator deity implies recognition of some type of difference between the creator and the created world, then Bādarāyaṇa's emphasis on the Brahman as creator can also be interpreted as an emphasis on the element of difference (*bheda*) in the God-world relationship.

The methodology employed in 1.1.16 of deducing one's position on the grounds that certain qualities are known to apply or not to apply to the subject under consideration, is one employed frequently by Bādarāyaṇa. Often the qualities referred to are not listed by Bādarāyaṇa, but rather must be found in the topical text. Hence, one method for investigating the theology held by Bādarāyaṇa is to identify the qualities to which he refers in the topical texts. In this case, that quality is creatorship.

Sūtra 1.1.17 presents another clear declaration of difference between the Brahman and the individual soul, with Bādarāyaṇa actually using the word '*bheda*' in the *sūtra*. Even the monist Śaṅkara agrees that this and the previous *sūtra* proclaim that the Highest Self (*Ātman*) and the individual soul (*jīva*) are different. Śaṅkara adds, however, that this difference only exists at the lower level of truth, and that ultimately there is only the one undifferentiated Brahman. Thus, he ends his commentary on 1.1.17 by declaring, 'With reference to this fictitious difference of the highest Self and the individual Self, the last two *sūtras* have been propounded.'[26] The absurdity of such an explanation of Bādarāyaṇa's *sūtras* is obvious, since *nowhere* in his entire work does Bādarāyaṇa make reference to two levels of truth. Śaṅkara is guilty of attaching his own doctrine onto the *Brahma*

Sūtras in order to make the work appear compatible with his non-dualist theology.

Difficulties in interpretation make the next *sūtra*, 1.1.18, rather ambiguous, although its content does not appear to be that significant, thereby minimizing the impact of this ambiguity on our overall analysis of Bādarāyaṇa's thought. Both Rāmānuja and Śaṅkara, for instance, offer reasonably convincing interpretations. According to Rāmānuja, the *sūtra* means that because the Blissful Self is said to create through desire and not with reference to that which is known through inference (i.e., Prime Matter), the Blissful Self must be the Highest Self, since the individual soul could only create through Prime Matter.[27] Śaṅkara interprets the *sūtra* as stating that because the Blissful Self creates through desire, the Blissful Self obviously is not Prime Matter, since the non-intelligent Prime Matter cannot experience 'desire' (*kāma*). Since our goal is not to evaluate the expositors' different interpretations of *sūtras* except where this is a necessary step in determining Bādarāyaṇa's original meaning, we shall forego a decision of whose interpretation of 1.1.18 is more accurate. The key point of this *sūtra*, however, is that once again Bādarāyaṇa speaks of the Brahman with reference to his role as *creator*, in this case creation through desire.

This topical section closes with another key *sūtra* in which Bādarāyaṇa reaffirms the difference between the Highest Self and the individual soul, but does so in a manner that also affirms some type of *identity*. Thus, for the first time, the doctrine of Difference-In-Identity appears in the *Brahma Sūtras*. More specifically, in *sūtra* 1.1.19 Bādarāyaṇa continues the affirmation of Difference found in the previous three *sūtras*, in this case pointing out that the topical text declares that the individual soul at liberation achieves a union (*yogam*) with the Blissful Self, the implication being that a union of two entities is possible only if there are indeed two distinct and different entities. At the same time, however, by affirming that the individual soul and the Blissful Self achieve a union, Bādarāyaṇa appears to advocate some type of Difference-In-Identity.

TOPIC SEVEN: THE SOLAR INDWELLER

1.1.20: *Antastaddharmopadeśāt*

The Golden Man standing in the sun is the Brahman, because He is declared to have the Brahman's attributes (as in the following passage: "Now that Golden Man seen within the sun—he has a golden beard, golden hair, and is all gold, to the tips of his nails. His eyes are like the red lotus. 'Up' is his name, becasue he is 'up' above all sin. One who knows him also rises up above all sin." *Chāndogya Upaniṣad* 1:6:6–7.)

1.1.21: *Bhedavyapadeśāccānyaḥ*

And, from declarations of difference, we know that there is another self, the soul (as in the passage: 'He Who stands in the sun, but is other than the sun; Whom the sun does not know, and Whose body the sun is; Who controls the sun from within—He is yourself, the controller of your soul, the immortal.' *Bṛhadāraṇyaka Upaniṣad* 3:7:9).

According to most expositors, this section address the topical text described above in 1.1.20. This text from the *Chāndogya Upaniṣad* describes the Golden Man who resides within the sun.

Madhva identifies a different source for the topical text (*Taittirīya Āraṇyaka* 3:2:24–25), but the content of the text is similar to that of the *Chāndogya Upaniṣad* passage, and Madhva's reading of Bādarāyaṇa's *sūtras* is similar to that of the other expositors.[28]

This section, like the preceding verse 1.1.19, appears to assert both Difference and Identity, although the precise manner in which they are combined is not here, or anywhere else in the *Brahma Sūtras*, clearly explained.

In 1.1.20, Bādarāyaṇa asserts that the Person (*puruṣa*) whom the *Chāndogya Upaniṣad* describes as residing within the sun must be the Brahman because of the qualities that are ascribed to that Person. Looking at the Upaniṣadic text, we see that that quality is 'freedom from sin.' By asserting that the Brahman is actually present within the sun, Bādarāyaṇa asserts some type of Identity. In the following *sūtra*, however, he significantly qualifies this Identity by declaring that the Brahman is *not* the deity who resides within the sun and who is, in a sense, the sun's individual soul. Bādarāyaṇa makes this statement on the basis of a 'declaration of difference' (*bhedavyapadeśāt*) which, according to Rāmānuja and Śaṅkara, comes from the *Bṛhadāraṇyaka Upaniṣad* passage cited above in the translation of *sūtra* 1.1.21.

Thus, Bādarāyaṇa clearly advocates Difference and Identity in this section by affirming that the Brahman dwells within the sun but is different from the deity who is the soul of the sun.

In terms of Bādarāyaṇa's methodology, it should be noted that in 1.1.20 he again uses the technique of proof through reference to qualities described in the topical text—qualities which, because their applicability to the Brahman is universally acknowledged, serve as proof that the object described by the qualities is indeed the Brahman. In this case, the quality referred to is 'freedom from sin,' an interesting quality in that it defines the difference between the Brahman and the rest of creation in *moral* terms, whereas most descriptions of the Brahman make reference to differences in power or ontological status (e.g., all-pervasiveness).

Before closing this section, reference should be made to Madhva's convincing explanation of the connection between this topical section and the previous one. Madhva has his opponent (*pūrvapakṣin*) raise the objection that in the previous section, the attributes ascribed to the Brahman could also belong to certain deities, since there are Upaniṣadic passages that attribute these qualities to deities. According to Madhva, Bādarāyaṇa responds in this section by pointing out that since the Brahman dwells within the deities, sometimes the texts use the names of the deities even though they actually are referring to Him, the supreme Brahman.[29]

TOPIC EIGHT: SPACE

1.1.22: *Ākāśastalliṅgāt*

The space mentioned in the Scriptures refers to the Brahman, because of the characteristic (of being the origin to things) ascribed to it (in passages such as those reporting the conversation between Pravāhaṇa Jaivali and Śilaka Śālavatya: 'To what does this world go back?' (asked Pravāhaṇa). 'To space,' said he (Śilaka). Verily here all things arise out of space. They disappear back into space, for space alone is greater than these; space is the final goal.' *Chāndogya Upaniṣad* 1:9:1).

The question addressed here is whether space (*ākāśa*) refers to the element of space or to the Brahman. The answer, again given by reference to a quality known to belong to the Brahman, is that space must refer to the Brahman since in the passage space is described as the source of the world and that to which the world returns.

TOPIC NINE: BREATH

1.1.23: *Āta eva prāṇaḥ*

For the same reason, the Scriptural passages on breath refer to the Brahman (passages like those where Uṣasti Cākrāyaṇa replies to the Prastotṛi priest's question 'Which is that divinity?' with the words 'Breath . . . Verily, indeed, all beings here enter (into life) with breath, and depart (from life) with breath.' *Chāndogya Upaniṣad* 1:11:5)

In other passages such as *Chāndogya Upaniṣad* 1:11:5, breath (prāṇa) is described in terms that suggest it is the highest principle. Do the passages refer to the element of breath, or is breath used to metaphorically refer to the Brahman? Bādarāyaṇa affirms the latter on the grounds that, as in the previous *sūtra*, the quality of being the source of life is ascribed to it—a quality that could only belong to the Brahman.

TOPIC TEN: LIGHT

1.1.24: *Jyotiścaraṇābhidhānāt*

The Brahman is the light spoken of in Scripture (which declares: 'Now the light which shines higher than this heaven, on the back of all, on the backs of everything, in the highest worlds, than which there are no higher—verily, this is the same as this light which is here within a person,' *Chāndogya Upaniṣad* 3:13:7), because of the mention of feet (or 'fourths') in a previous passage of the same scripture which reads: 'all beings are one foot (or one fourth) of Him. The three feet (or fourths), are in heaven.' *Chāndogya Upaniṣad* 3:12:6).

1.1.25: *Chando'bhidhānānneti cenna tathā ceto 'rpaṇanigadāt tathāhi darśanam*

As the latter passage alludes to the Gāyatrī metre, can it be then the Brahman is not referred to?

No, because the allusion to the Gāyatrī is only to facilitate meditation on the Brahman.

1.1.26: *Bhūtādipādavyapadeśopapatteścaivam*

And the statement that all beings form a foot (quarter) of the Gāyatrī is meaningful only if the Gāyatrī refers to the Brahman.

1.1.27: *Upadeśabhedānneti cennobhayasminnapyavirodhāt*

The Brahman cannot be the subject of both descriptions ('in heaven,' *Chāndogya Upaniṣad* 3:12:6) and 'higher than this heaven' *Chāndogya Upaniṣad* 3:13:7.)

Not true, for, immense as it is, the Brahman can be in both regions without contradiction.

Bādarāyaṇa now proceeds to demonstrate that the Scriptural texts which refer to light actually refer to the Brahman, and not to the element of light.

Consideration is given to a passage in the *Chāndogya Upaniṣad* 3:13:7) in which light is described in very grandiose terms:

> Now the light which shines higher than this heaven, on the backs of all, on the backs of everything, in the highest worlds, than which there are no higher—verily, this is the same as this light which is here within a person.

Bādarāyaṇa argues that the Brahman is meant by this reference to light, since an earlier passage in the section clearly indicates that the Brahman is the topic. In this passage, all beings are referred to as the feet of the Gāyatrī metre. Bādarāyaṇa's point is that since only the Brahman could have all beings as its feet, then the Gāyatrī must actually refer to Him. In 1.1.25, Bādarāyaṇa explains this rather unusual manner of using one name (Gāyatrī) to refer to another (Brahman) on the grounds that such an identification is often made for the purpose of facilitating meditation.[30]

In 1.1.26, Bādarāyaṇa seems to repeat the point made in 1.1.24, namely that the Gāyatrī must refer to the Brahman since only He could have all beings for his feet. Such redundancy, however, would appear to be out of character for a work as orderly as the *Brahma Sūtras*. Hence, we are inclined to accept Madhva's analysis that 1.1.24 is a separate topic dealing with light, while 1.1.25 to 27 is another topic dealing with the Gāyatrī. Madhva also argues that while the topics through 1.1.24 deal with finite realities that refer to the Brahman (i.e., space, breath and light), the following topics examine eternal realities that refer to the Brahman.[31]

The section closes with 1.1.27, in which an objection is presented that the Brahman cannot be the subject of both the passage on the

Gāyatrī, where the subject is said to be *in* Heaven, and the passage on light, where the subject is said to be *above* Heaven. Bādarāyaṇa responds that in fact there is no contradiction between the two passages, though it is left to the expositors to explain away this apparent contradiction. Rāmānuja and Śaṅkara, for example, remark that 'in' and 'above' are used interchangeably, as in the case of a bird sitting on top of a tree, which can be described as both 'in' and 'above' the tree. One could also respond to the objection by pointing out that as an omnipresent being, the Brahman can be described as simultaneously 'in' and 'above' anything.

There are, of course, many aspects of this topical section that we have interpreted with reference to ideas presented by the expositors: indeed, we shall see that the meaning of many verses of the *Brahma Sūtras* remains elusive unless the expositors are consulted. Nonetheless, if we attempt to strip away the expositors' interpretations and look only at what can be deduced from Bādarāyaṇa's own words, we are again inclined to see an assertion of some type of limited Identity between the Brahman and the world. Bādarāyaṇa's own words appear to declare that light and the Gāyatrī are used to refer to the Brahman. In order to be used in this manner, the necessary presupposition is some type of close connection—though certainly not pure Identity—with the Brahman. Hence, we are left with another hint that Bādarāyaṇa advocates some type of Difference-In-Identity.

TOPIC ELEVEN: INDRA AS BREATH

1.1.28: *Prāṇastathānugamāt*

The breath to which Scripture alludes (as in the passage, "Then Indra said, 'I am the breath, the Intelligent Self. As such reverence me as life, as Immortality,'" *Kauṣītāki Upaniṣad* 3:2), is the Brahman because of the connection with words that could only denote the Brahman. *Kauṣītaki Upaniṣad* 3:2.).

1.1.29: *Na vakturātmopadeśāditi*
cedadhyātmasambandhabhūmā hyasmin

The breath is arguably not the Brahman, because the speaker, Indra, is referring it to himself (and thus identifying himself with it.)

This is denied, since in the passage in question, there is much to connect the breath with the Highest Self (as the attribute of immortality, which is the Brahman's alone.)

1.1.30: *Śāstradṛṣṭyā tūpadeśo vāmadevavat*

That self-identificatory reference of Indra's accords with Scripture's way of speaking, as in the instance of Vāmadeva (with regard to whom Scripture declares: "Brahman, indeed, was this from the beginning. It knew itself only as 'I am the Brahman'." Therefore it became all. Whoever among the gods awakened to this, he, indeed, became that. It is the same in the case of seers, the same in the case of men. Seeing this, indeed, the seer Vāmadeva knew 'I was Manu, and the sun too'. *Bṛhadāraṇyaka Upaniṣad* 1:4:10.)

1.1.31: *Jīvamukhyaprāṇaliṅgānneti*
cennopāsātraividhyādāśritatvādiha tadyogāt

Might it be that Scripture here is not speaking of the Brahman, because what is described is linked with the soul (as in the words 'speech is not what one should desire to understand, one should know the speaker,' *Kauṣītaki Upaniṣad* 3:8), and with the chief breath (as in the words: 'But now, it is the breathing spirit alone, the intelligent self that seizes hold of this body and makes it rise up' *Ibid.* 3:3)?

Not so, because then there would be three types of meditation, because our own view of the identity of the breath with the Brahman is seen elsewhere, and because the characteristics spoken of in the passage are conformable to the Brahman.

Bādarāyaṇa next examines Scriptural texts in which Indra, identifying himself as breath (*prāṇa*), makes several statements indicating that he, not the Brahman, is the highest being. The topical text comes from the *Kauṣītakī Upaniṣad* 3:2:

> Then Indra said: 'I am the breath, the intelligent self. As such, reverence me as life, as immortality.'

Madhva chooses a topical text from the *Aitareya Āraṇyaka*, but the content appears to be similar to that of the *Kauṣītakī Upaniṣad*.[32]

There are several possible interpretations of 1.1.28, but the most likely one declares that breath (and Indra) refer to the Brahman because of the connection of breath with words that could only describe the Brahman. This is a technique that we previously have seen Bādarāyaṇa employ in 1.1.16, 1.1.20, 1.1.22, and 1.1.23. The qualities referred to in this case include being immortal and granting immortality to others.

While this is the second *sūtra* in which the topic of breath is discussed (the other being 1.1.23), Bādarāyaṇa is not being redundant here, since the actual topic of this section is Indra, who refers to himself as breath.

Sūtra 1.1.29 posits a strong challenge to Bādarāyaṇa's interpretation of the topical text: how can it be said that the Brahman is the subject of the passage when Indra clearly refers to *himself*? Bādarāyaṇa's response is found in the second half of this *sūtra*, and then again in the following two *sūtras*. His response in the second half of 1.1.29 is rather unclear, but he appears to be stating that the numerous references in the passage to what could only be the Highest Self demand an interpretation that Indra is not the true subject. Or, as Madhva suggests, Bādarāyaṇa might be arguing that because Indra experiences such a close connection with the Highest Self (*ātmasambandhabhūmā*), he is at liberty to identify himself with the Brahman, even though the identity is not real. Madhva's interpretation recommends itself on the grounds that the alternative interpretation would be essentially a repetition of 1.1.28.[33]

Madhva's interpretation gains further credence when we examine 1.1.30, where Bādarāyaṇa more clearly asserts that Indra can identify himself with the Brahman as a result of the wisdom he attained through Scripture. Bādarāyaṇa cites the comparable case of Vāmadeva, described in the *Bṛhadāraṇyaka Upaniṣad* 1:4:10, where upon hearing that the Brahman became the All, he declares: 'I was Manu and the Sun.'

This is, of course, an exceptionally important *sūtra*, in that it acknowledges the validity of one of Scripture's strongest statements on Identity. Bādarāyaṇa, unfortunately, does not elaborate on the specific nature of this Identity (in contrast, for example, to Rāmānuja and Śaṅkara, who use this *sūtra* as an opportunity to present lengthy descriptions of their own views on Identity), but at least he clearly acknowledges a belief in *some* type of Identity.

This topical section concludes with 1.1.31, an unusually long *sūtra* that offers three more reasons against interpreting Indra and breath as not referring to the Brahman: first, there would result a Scriptural injunction to meditate on three different objects; secondly, the view that breath refers to the Brahman is confirmed elsewhere; and thirdly, qualities described in the text can refer only to the Brahman.

This topic ends the first section (*pāda*) of the first chapter (*adhyāya*) of the *Brahma Sūtras*. With reference to our attempt to identify Bādarāyaṇa's own theology, the first topic has provided us with the following insights:

1. Bādarāyaṇa understands the Brahman as a being with qualities.
2. Perhaps the most important of these qualities is that of being creator of the world.
3. The Brahman is in some sense different from His creation.
4. Yet at the same time, He in some sense shares Identity with His creation.

FOOTNOTES

1. See above, pp. 16-22.
2. Ghate, *The Vedānta*, p. 54.
3. Monier Monier-Williams, *A Sanskrit-English Dictionary* (Delhi: Motilal Banarsidass, 1989), p. 17.
4. See, for example, the opening *sūtra* of Patñjali in Pereira, *Hindu Theology*, p. 78.
5. Thibaut, trans., *The Vedānta Sūtras with Commentary by Śaṅkara,* 1:12.
6. Ghate, *The Vedānta*, p. 53.
7. B.N.K. Sharma, *The Brahma Sūtras,* 1:57.
8. See *sūtras* 1.2.31, 1.3.31, 1.4.18, 3.2.40, 3.4.2, 3.4.18, 3.4.40, 4.3.12, 4.4.5, and 4.4.11.
9. Thus, for example, in his *Śatadūsaṇī* (*The Hundred Refutations of Nondualism*), Vedānta Deśika comments on Bādarāyaṇa's first *sūtra*:

> The aphorism "Now then is the enquiry into (or the desire to know) the Brahman," does not accord with the Nondualist position, for its Absolute Consciousness (or the Brahman), as self-illuminant, is not an object of knowledge (especially of an awareness other than its own. In all knowledge the knowing subject, the illuminator, is distinct from the known object, the illuminated). A desire to know the Brahman is therefore unjustified. But if the Brahman becomes an object of knowledge, through being qualified by superimposed qualities and forms, since such are matured by Ignorance, the desire to know the Brahman will a fortiori be unjustified (as what is known will be a delusion).
>
> [Śri Kanch: P.B. Annangaracharyar, ed., *Śrīmadvedāntadeśikagranthamālā* (Conjeevaram: Granthamala Office, 1940), 1:242).

10. The doctrine of two levels of truth is clearly Buddhist doctrine, nowhere better formulated than by Nāgārguna himself in the *Mādhyamikaśāstra* 24:8-10:

> The doctrinal instruction of the Buddha is founded on two truths: the common sensible obfuscatory (or Relative) Truth and the Truth Supreme (or Absolute). Those who do not comprehend the separation of these two truths do not comprehend the profundity of the Buddhist doctrine. Without recourse to the

empirical, the absolute cannot be taught; without the attainment of Absolute Truth, nirvāṇa cannot be realized (translation by Jose Pereira).

11. Das Gupta, *History of Indian Philosophy*, 4:122.
12. Radhakrishnan, *Brahma Sūtras*, p. 237.
13. Das Gupta, *History of Indian Philosophy*, 4:121.
14. Thibaut, trans., *The Vedānta Sūtras with Commentary by Śaṅkara*, 1:20.
15. B.N.K. Sharma, *The Brahma Sūtras*, 1:81–82.
16. Thibaut, trans., *The Vedānta Sūtras with The Commentary of Rāmānuja*, p. 161.
17. Radhakrishnan, *The Brahma Sūtras*, pp. 246–247.
18. B.N.K. Sharma, *The Brahma Sūtras*, 1:22–23.
19. Savrepalli Radhakrishnan and Charles A. Moore, eds., *A Source-book in Indian Philosophy* (Princeton: Princeton University Press, 1957), pp. 424–452.
20. This interpretation runs closest to that of Rāmānuja and Nimbārka. For Śaṅkara's version, based on the concept of *Arundhatīnyāya*, see Thibaut, trans., *Vedānta Sūtras with Commentary by Śaṅkara*, 1:57–60.
21. B.N.K. Sharma, *The Brahma Sūtras*, 1:91.
22. Radhakrishnan, *The Brahma Sūtras*, p. 253.
23. Das Gupta agrees that Madhva's position is the more convicing. See Das Gupta, *History of Indian Philosophy*, 4:129–130.
24. See Appendix C.
25. See the remarks of Ghate, *The Vedānta*, p. 55.
26. Thibaut, trans., *The Vedānta Sūtras with Commentary by Śaṅkara*, 1:70.
27. Thibaut, trans., *The Vedānta Sūtras with The Commentary by Rāmānuja*, p. 236.
28. B.N.K. Sharma, *The Brahma Sūtras*, 1:111–115.
29. Ibid.
30. The technique of proving that a words refers to the Brahman by declaring that the word is used to facilitate meditation is used on several occasions by Bādarāyaṇa. It is a rather suspect technique, in that one could employ it to prove that *any* word refers to the Brahman.
31. B.N.K. Sharma, *The Brahma Sūtras*, 1:122–129.
32. Ibid., 1:126.
33. An objective inquirer might draw the conclusion that Indra's identification of himself as the highest God should be taken literally, and was written by a sect which worshipped Indra as such. Unfortunately, the Hindu interpreters are bound by the doctrine that all Scripture is divinely revealed and expresses one truth, and hence are compelled to make even the most unlikely passages appear to refer to the Brahman.

CHAPTER V

An Analysis of the *Brahma Sūtras* 1:2

TOPIC ONE: THE BEING CONSISTING OF MIND

1.2.1: *Savatraprasiddhopadeśāt*

The being which consists of mind is the Brahman, because the teaching about it is established everywhere (in Scripture, especially in *Chāndogya Upaniṣad* 3:14, which reads: 'Verily this whole world is the Brahman, from which he comes forth, without which he will be dissovled, and in which he breathes. Tranquil, one should meditate on it . . . He who consists of mind, whose body is life, whose form is light, whose conception is truth, whose soul is space, containing all works, containing all desires, containing all odours, containing all tastes, encompassing this whole world, being without speech and without concern. This is my self within the heart, smaller than a grain of rice, than a barley corn, than a mustard seed, than a grain of millet or than the kernel of a grain of millet. This is my self within the heart, greater than the earth, greater than the atmosphere, greater than the sky, greater than these worlds . . . into him I shall enter, on departing hence. Verily, he who believes this, will have no more doubt.'

1.2.2: *Vivakṣitaguṇopapatteśca*

This being is the Brahman, because the qualities described in the above passage conform to it.

1.2.3: *Anupapattestu na śārīraḥ*

This being is not the embodied soul: (a) because those qualities do not conform to it.

1.2.4: *Karmakartṛvyapadeśācca*

(b) Because the passage speaks of agent and object of action. (It speaks of an object to be entered, the Brahman, and of the one who is to enter it, the soul, in the line 'Into him I shall enter, on departing hence'.)

1.2.5: *Śabdaviśeṣāt*

(c) Because the words used to describe the soul and the Brahman are different. (The above passage describes the Brahman as 'He who consists of mind, whose body is life, whose form is light' etc.; and the soul as 'This is myself within the heart, smaller than a grain of rice, than a barley corn,' etc.)

1.2.6: *Smṛteśca*

And (d) because sacred tradition also proclaims this difference (as for instance, the *Gītā*, with these words: 'The Lord resides in the hearts of all beings, Arjuna, causing all beings to whirl around by this wondrous power as though mounted on a machine.' 18:61).

1.2.7: *Arbhakaukastvāt tadvyapadeśācca netī cenna niccāyatvādevam vyomavacca*

As the abode is a small one (described in the words, 'This is my self within the heart') and its smallness remarked upon (in the words 'smaller than a grain of rice, than a barley corn, than a mustard seed'), can it be that the passage is not about the Brahman (who is infinite), but about the soul, (which is infinitesimal)?

No. The reference to smallness is to facilitate meditation, and the Brahman is like space (pervading the infinite and the infinitesimal at once).

1.2.8: *Saṃbhogaprāptiriti cenna vaiśeṣyāt*

If it abides in the soul, will not the Brahman (like the soul), experience pleasure and pain?

No, because the Brahman and the soul are different.

The second section (*pāda*) of the first chapter (*adhyāya*) begins with an eight verse topic. According to Śaṅkara, this section examines Scriptural passages which do not clearly refer to the Brahman. Rāmānuja sees this section as addressing passages which on the surface appear to refer to the individual soul. Madhva believes that the section looks at passages which appear to refer to things other than the Brahman. In any case, the first topic of this section is an important one, since it offers a further glimpse at Bādarāyaṇa's own theology.

The topical text identified by most expositors is found in *Chāndogya Upaniṣad* 3:14, and quoted above in the translation of *sūtra* 1.2.1. The question arises as to the identity of the person who consists of mind (*manomaya*): is it the individual soul or the Supreme Self, the Brahman? In 1.2.1, Bādarāyaṇa affirms that the reference is to the Brahman, since 'this teaching is well-known everywhere.'

Unfortunately, this *sūtra* offers a fine illustration of the difficulties encountered in arriving at a reasonably accurate account of Bādarāyaṇa's intended meaning. There is, for instance, no subject identified in the three word compound of Bādarāyaṇa's *sūtra.* Literally, the *sūtra* means 'because it is well-known everywhere.' Bādarāyaṇa himself does not offer any indication as to *what* is 'well-known everywhere.' This crucial information must be derived from the topical text which, of course, is not given to us by Bādaryāyaṇa.

This *sūtra* also serves as an example of the rather weak methods of proof that Bādarāyaṇa sometimes employs to establish his points. To state that something must be true because it is commonly believed to be true by most people is hardly a very sound method of theologizing, yet it is a method that Bādarāyaṇa uses on several occasions.

In further establishing his position, Bādarāyaṇa proceeds with a series of *sūtras* which, like 1.1.6 to 1.1.19, seem to suggest a very strong belief in the difference between the Brahman and the individual soul. In 1.2.2, he argues that the person consisting of mind must refer to the Brahman since qualities attributed to it could only apply to the Brahman. The converse is stated in 1.2.3, namely that the reference must be to the Brahman since the qualities listed in the passage could not apply to an embodied soul. Some of the qualities listed in the passage to which Bādarāyaṇa apparently is referring include: containing all works, desires, tastes, and odours; emcompassing the whole world; and being greater than the worlds.

In 1.2.4, Bādarāyaṇa adopts a different approach by defending his identification of *manomaya* with the Brahman through reference to another part of the passage. Specifically, he refers to *Chāndogya Upaniṣad* 3:14:4, where it states, 'Into him I shall enter on departing hence.' Bādarāyaṇa argues that this passage distinguishes between the soul as actor and the Brahman as the object of the soul's action, such distinction implying a difference between the Brahman and the individual soul.

Sūtra 1.2.5 again affirms difference between the Brahman and the individual soul on the basis that they are referred to by different words in the text.

The sixth *sūtra* declares that Sacred Tradition (*Smṛti*) also describes the Brahman and the individual soul as different. Bādarāyaṇa, of course, does not identify which Sacred Traditions offer such a description, but Rāmānuja refers to the *Bhagavad Gītā* 15:19 and both Rāmānuja and Śaṅkara (as well as the theologians of the Nimbārka school) refer to the *Bhagavad Gītā* 18:61, both of which differentiate between devotee and object of devotion.

Consistent with our earlier observation that Bādarāyaṇa advocates both Difference *and* Identity, we now see him move from five *sūtras* affirming Difference to, in 1.2.7, a *sūtra* affirming immanence, and hence some type of Identity. This *sūtra* addresses the section of the topical text which describes the person consisting of mind as 'smaller than a grain of rice' and residing within the heart. The objection is raised that such attributes of smallness could not possibly refer to the almighty Brahman. Bādarāyaṇa responds that such descriptions of the Brahman are indeed appropriate since, first of all, the Brahman is described as dwelling in the heart in a figurative sense for the purpose of aiding meditation, and secondly, since the Brahman is all-pervasive like space, He can be said to reside anywhere, including the small space within the heart. By affirming this doctrine of immanence **in which the Brahman resides within the soul, which, presumably,** remains a separate and distinct being, Bādarāyaṇa appears to advocate a type of Difference-In-Identity similar to the Qualified Non-dualism of Rāmānuja.

The closing *sūtra* of this section responds to the argument that if the Brahman dwells within the heart, he therefore must experience the individual's pleasure and pain. Bādarāyaṇa responds that this is not so since even though the Brahman dwells in the heart, he remains different from the individual soul. This, of course, brings to mind the famous section in the *Bṛhadāraṇyaka Upaniṣad* where the Brahman is described as 'dwelling in' but 'other than' the individual soul and other finite realities.

We see, then, in this section further indications that Bādarāyaṇa believes in both Difference and Identity. He repeatedly asserts that the soul is different from the Brahman, often asserting the Brahman's superiority by stating that certain wonderful qualities ascribed to Him could never apply to the individual soul. At the same time, he advocates a type of Identity in which the Brahman resides in all of His creation. Note that at no point has Bādarāyaṇa questioned the reality of the soul: rather, he seems to accept it as a separate, though dependent, reality. Hence, both the Brahman and the creation are real and distinct (Difference), yet the Brahman dwells within the creation (Identity). This is obviously quite similar to the positions of Rāmānuja, Nimbārka, and even Madhva, and quite different from the position of Śaṅkara, who attempts to explain away those of Bādarāyaṇa's *sūtras* which affirm Difference on the grounds that they are stated at the lower level of truth. The obvious objection to this practice of Śaṅkara is that the doctrine of two levels of truth is not propounded by Bādarāyaṇa anywhere in the *Brahma Sūtras*. Instead, it appears to be a doctrine which Śaṅkara reads into the *Brahma Sūtras* in order to make them appear to be compatible with his own Monist philosophy.

TOPIC TWO: THE EATER

1.2.9: *Attā carācaragrahaṇāt*

The Brahman is the eater, because He devours the movable and the unmoving. (As Scripture declares: 'Who knows where He is the God for whom both the Brahmin (the unmoving) and the warrior (the movable) are rice, and Death the sauce?' *Kaṭha Upaniṣad* 2:25).

1.2.10: *Prakaraṇācca*

Furthermore, the Brahman is the topic under discussion in the Scriptural passage quoted.

Bādarāyaṇa now examines a question raised by the topical text in *Kaṭha Upaniṣad* 2:25; namely whether this being referred to as consuming the living and the dead is the Brahman or an individual soul. Bādarāyaṇa responds that the reference must be to the Brahman, since only He is great enough to be identified as consuming all creation. *Sūtra* 1.2.10 confirms this position by pointing out that earlier verses in the same section of the *Kaṭha Upaniṣad* indicate the Brahman is the topic under discussion.

In terms of identifying Bādarāyaṇa's theology, this section suggests a belief in some type of difference between the Brahman and the world, in that the Brahman can only seize or 'take in' (*grahaṇa*) the world of moving and non-moving beings if He is in some sense separate from them. At the same time, however, such 'taking in' implies some type of union between distinct entities, and hence suggests a Difference-In-Identity theology similar to that of Rāmānuja and Nimbārka, or even the Difference theology of Madhva which in many ways resembles the Difference-In-Identity of Nimbārka and Rāmānuja, inasmuch as all three believe that the world and the Brahman are eternally distinct but intimately united in the state of release.

TOPIC THREE: THE TWO PERSONS IN THE CAVE

1.2.11: *Guhām praviṣṭāvātmānau hi taddarśanāt*

The two selves who have entered the cave (whom Scripture describes in the passage: 'There are two selves that drink the fruit of righteousness in the world of good deeds. Both are lodged in the cave (of the heart), in the highest upper sphere'), are the soul and the Brahman, because this meaning is evident (in the same Scripture, where the text: 'Realizing through self that primal God, difficult to be seen, deeply hidden, set in the cave, dwelling in the deep, the wise man leaves behind both joy and sorrow' *Kaṭha Upaniṣad* 2:12, clearly refers to the Brahman; and the lines: 'She who arises with life, Aditi, the soul of the gods, who stands, having entered the cave, who was born with the beings' *Kaṭha Upaniṣad* 4:7, can be interpreted to refer to the soul).

1.2.12: *Viśeṣaṇācca*

And because the two are differentiated (in their characteristics, as of the one, who is liberated, 'the wise man leaves behind both joy and sorrow' and the other, the goal of liberation itself: 'Realizing through self, that primal God, difficult to be seen, deeply hidden, set in the cave, dwelling in the deep').

This section examines another text in the same Upaniṣad, *Kaṭha Upaniṣad* 3:1, where two beings are described as residing within the cave in the heart.

For a change, in this *sūtra* Bādarāyaṇa clearly identifies the subject, namely the two selves who have entered the cave in the heart (*guhām praviṣṭāvātmānau*). Unfortunately, he does not employ such clarity in helping us identify these two selves, since the only reason he offers for making such an identification is *'darśanāt'*, which is interpreted differently by Śaṅkara, Rāmānuja, and Madhva. Śaṅkara and Rāmānuja believe that the two selves refer to the individual soul and the Highest Self, while Madhva believes that they refer to two forms of the Brahman.[1] While Madhva offers a lengthy and fairly convincing justification of his position, we are inclined to accept the interpretation of Rāmānuja and Śaṅkara on the grounds that it lets this section fit in well with surrounding sections that suggest some type of Difference-In-Identity. Bādarāyaṇa's use of the dual *ātmānau* clearly refer to *two* different beings, yet by describing them as residing together in the cave in the heart, a type of union also is affirmed.

The second *sūtra* of this section employs Bādarāyaṇa's commonly used technique of proving his point by demonstrating that the qualities described in the Scriptural passage indicate that the reference must be to that which he says it is, which in this case, according to Rāmānuja and Śaṅkara, is to both the individual soul and the Highest Self. Madhva, however, argues that the qualities described in Scripture affirm his position that the reference is to two forms of the Brahman.

Finally, it should be noted that Rāmānuja does not treat these two *sūtras* as a separate topic, but instead considers them an extension of the previous topic.

TOPIC FOUR: THE PERSON WITHIN THE EYE

1.2.13: *Antara upapatteḥ*

The person in the eye of whom Scripture speaks (in the passage, 'That Person who is seen in the eye—he is the self. That is the immortal, the fearless. That is the Brahman.' *Chāndogya Upaniṣad* 4:15:1) is the Brahman, because the qualities of this person are applicable to the Brahman.

1.2.14: *Sthānādivyapadeśācca*

And because Scripture speaks of the Brahman as abiding in a place, the eye, the person in the eye is the Brahman and no other.

1.2.15: *Sukhaviśiṣṭābhidhānādeva ca*

And because that person is the same as the other earlier described by Scripture as qualified by joy (in the lines 'Life is the Brahman, joy is the Brahman, ether is the Brahman.' *Chāndogya Upaniṣad* 4:10:4).

1.2.15a: *Ata eva ca sabrahma*

And for that same reason, ether is the Brahman.

1.2.16: *Śrutopaniṣatkagatyabhidhānācca*

And also because the path of that person is the same as that of the man who has listened to the Upaniṣad (a path described by Scripture in the words, 'But those who seek the path of the Self by austerity, chastity, faith, and knowledge, they, by the Northern route, gain the sun. That, verily, is the support of life breaths. That is eternal, the fearless. That is the final goal. From that they do not return.' *Praśna Upaniṣad* 1:10).

1.2.17: *Anavastitherasambhavācca netaraḥ*

The person in the eye can be none other than the Brahman because of the impermanence of all other selves and because of the impossibility of other selves possessing the qualities attributed to the person in the eye (such qualities like immortality and fearlessness, mentioned in the topical text).

In the *Chāndogya Upaniṣad* 4:15:1, we read about a person residing in the eye:

> 'That Person who is seen in the eye—he is the Self,' said he.
>
> 'That is the immortal, the fearless. That is the Brahman. So even if they pour clarified butter or water on that, it goes away to the edges.'

Bādarāyaṇa addresses the question of the identity of this person: is it the individual soul, a deity, or the Brahman? Bādarāyaṇa answers in 1.2.13 that it is the Brahman, since the qualities described in the text could belong only to Him. As usual, Bādarāyaṇa does not list these qualities, but an examination of the topical text and following verses reveals such descriptions as immortal, fearless, and shining in all worlds.

In 1.2.14 Bādarāyaṇa provides further support for his position by referring to another passage in Scripture where the Brahman is described as abiding in the eye. Bādarāyaṇa does not list the specific passage, but Rāmānuja refers to *Bṛhadāraṇyaka Upaniṣad* 3:7:18: 'He who, dwelling in the eye, yet is other than the eye . . . He is the Self, the Inner Controller, the Immortal.'

In 1.2.15, Bādarāyaṇa again calls on other Scriptural passages to support his position. The person in the eye was earlier described (*Chāndogya Upaniṣad* 4:10:4) as qualified by pleasure (*ka*), and since the being qualified by pleasure is declared to be the Brahman, the person in the eye must be the Brahman, too. Rāmānuja and Nimbārka insert another *sūtra* at this point, based on the same text describing *ka* and *kha* (space). Since the other expositors do not include this *sūtra*, and since it represents a digression from the topic of the person in the sun, we assume it is not one of Bādarāyaṇa's own *sūtras*.

In 1.2.16, Bādarāyaṇa argues that the person in the eye must be the Brahman since the path to this person resembles the path to the Brahman. Finally, Bādarāyaṇa closes the topic in 1.2.17 by, according to Śaṅkara and Rāmānuja, stating that the person in the eye cannot be an individual since individual selves only reside there impermanently, and since the qualities ascribed to the person in the eye do not apply to the individual self. Madhva, in contrast, sees this *sūtra* as rejecting the idea that Agni is the person residing in the eye. Since Rāmānuja's and Śaṅkara's interpretation in part reports what has already been stated in 1.2.13, we are inclined to accept Madhva's position.

With reference to Bādarāyaṇa's theology, this section offers us two hints. On the one hand, by identifying the Brahman as the person in the eye, Bādarāyaṇa accepts one of the Upaniṣads' strongest statements on immanence. On the other hand, by arguing that the person residing in the eye is not the individual soul or a deity, Bādarāyaṇa appears to assert an immanence in which Difference is maintained. This, of course, is consistent with the position that we have detected in Bādarāyaṇa's previous topics.

TOPIC FIVE: THE INNER CONTROLLER

1.2.18: *Antaryāmyadhidaivādiṣu taddharmavyapadeśāt*

The Inner Controller of the gods and other beings (of whom

Scripture speaks in passages like: 'He who dwells in all beings, yet is other than all beings, whom no beings know, whose body is all beings, who controls all beings from within, he is your self, the Inner Controller, the Immortal,' *Bṛhadāraṇyaka Upaniṣad* 3:7:15) is the Brahman, because the Brahman's qualities are ascribed to it (qualities such as controlling from within, of the phenomena of the physical world like earth, water, fire, atmosphere, wind, sky, sun, the quarters, moon, stars, ether, darkness and light; and phenomena connected with the Self like breath, speech, sight, hearing, thinking, touch, knowledge and generative power).

1.2.19: *Na ca smārtamataddharmābhilāpāt*

The Inner Controller is not what tradition (like that of the Sāṅkhyas) says it is, (Prime Matter), because the latter lacks the qualities that the Scriptural passage predicates of it (attributes, such as those of seeing, hearing and thinking, which are those of a conscious being, while Prime Matter is an unconscious substance).

1.2.20: *Śārīraścobhaye' pi hi bhedenainamadhīyate*

The Inner Controller is not the individual soul in both recensions of the Scriptural text (*Bṛhadāraṇyaka Upaniṣad* 8:7:22; that of the Mādhyandins reads, 'He who dwells in the self,' and that of the Kāṇvas, 'He who dwells in the understanding') because both show soul and indwelling controller to be different (as the words themselves demonstrate: 'He who dwells in the self/understanding, yet is other than the self/understanding, whom the self/understanding does not know, whose body the self/understanding is, who controls the self/understanding from within, he is your self, the Inner Controller, the Immortal').

Bādarāyaṇa's next series of *sūtras* is based on the topical text found in the *Bṛhadāraṇyaka Upaniṣad* 3:7. This is one of the most well-known sections of the Upaniṣads, and has served as the basis for Rāmānuja's soul-body analogy that is the hallmark of his Qualified Non-dualism. The text speaks of an Inner Controller (*antaryāmin*) who 'dwells in' all of creation but at the same time is 'other than' that in which He dwells. Thus, for example:

> He who, dwelling in the earth, yet is other than the earth, whom the earth does not know, whose body the earth is, who controls the earth from within—He is your Soul, the Inner Controller, the Immortal.

This same description of the Inner Controller is made with reference to residing in the waters, fire, air, wind, sky, sun, the heavens, the moon and stars, space, darkness, light, all things, breath, speech, the eye, the ear, the mind, the skin, the understanding, and the semen.

In the three *sūtras* of this section, Bādarāyaṇa appears to assert that: (1) the Inner Controller is the Brahman (1.2.18); (2) the Inner Controller is not Prime Matter (1.2.19); and (3) the Inner Controller is not the individual soul (1.2.20). Consequently, Bādarāyaṇa strongly asserts the Difference between the Brahman and creation, while at the same time acknowledging that the Brahman dwells within the creation.

Sūtra 1.2.18 states that the Inner Controller refers to the Brahman, since the qualities ascribed to the Inner Controller could only belong to Him. Again, Bādarāyaṇa neglects to include these qualities in the *sūtra*, but in the topical text we find that the Inner Controller is described as the ruler of all worlds, a quality possessed only by the Brahman. It should be noted that Rāmānuja and Nimbārka add '*adhiloka*' to the first compound of Bādarāyaṇa's *sūtra*, making it read 'Inner Controller of the gods, worlds, etc.'

In 1.2.19, reference is made to 'that which is described in Sacred Tradition,' an expression used by Bādarāyaṇa on several occasions to refer to the Sāṅkhyan category of Prime Matter. Bādarāyaṇa declares that the Inner Controller is not Prime Matter, again due to the qualities applied to the Inner Controller by Scripture. The Scriptural reference apparently is to the passage in the topical text which describes the Inner Controller as the 'unseen Seer, unheard Hearer, unthought Thinker, and ununderstood Understander.' The negative adjectives (unheard, unseen, etc.) could be descriptions of the impersonal, unconscious Prime Matter. However, Bādarāyaṇa points out that the positive words (seer, hearer, etc.) express traits that could only apply to a conscious being, and never to Prime Matter which is unconscious.

According to Rāmānuja and Nimbārka, the words *sārīraś ca* are included in 1.2.19, and indicate that the individual soul is not meant by the Inner Controller. Śaṅkara and Madhva, on the other hand, include these words at the beginning of 1.2.20, but offer the same interpretation. All of the expositors, however, agree that *ubhaye* refers to 'both' recensions of the Bṛhadāraṇyaka passage, the meaning being that in both the Kāṇva and Mādhyandin recensions, the individual soul is described as different from the Inner Controller.

This topical section provides us with even further evidence that Bādarāyaṇa's own theology is one which contains both Difference and Identity. That the Inner Controller is not the individual soul or Prime Matter clearly asserts an element of Difference; but the fact that the Inner Controller resides in these, and indeed, *all* realities, strongly asserts an element of Identity.

TOPIC SIX: THE INVISIBLE

1.2.21: *Adṛśyatvādiguṇako dharmokteḥ*

The being endowed with qualities like invisibility described in Scripture (in passages like: 'That which is invisible, ungraspable... without sight or hearing... without hand or foot, eternal, all-pervading, omnipresent, exceedingly subtle; that is the Imperishable, which the wise perceive as the source of being.' *Muṇḍaka Upaniṣad* 1:6) is the Brahman, because the qualities ascribed to it, as being 'all-pervading' and 'the source of being' are the Brahman's alone.

1.2.22: *Viśeṣaṇabhedavyapadeśābhyām ca netarau*

Such a being cannot be identified with the other two basic categories of reality, Prime Matter and the soul, becasue distinctive and differential attributes are ascribed to it (distinctive, like being 'all-pervading,' and differential, like being 'higher than the highest immutable,' *Muṇḍaka Upaniṣad* 2:1:2).

1.2.23: *Rūpopanyāsācca*

And because Scripture describes the being's form (which is clearly that of the Brahman, with the words: 'Fire is His head, His eyes are the sun and the moon, the regions of space are His ears, His speech the revealed Vedas; air is His life and His heart the world. Out of His feet the earth (is born); indeed, He is the self of all beings.' *Muṇḍaka Upaniṣad* 2:1:4).

The topical text for this section is *Muṇḍaka Upaniṣad* 1:6:

> That which is invisible, ungraspable, without family, without caste,
> Without sight or hearing is It, without hand or foot,
> Eternal, all-pervading, omnipresent, exceedingly subtle;

That is the Imperishable, which the wise perceive as the source of being.

In 1.2.21, Bādarāyaṇa states that the invisible being is the Brahman, and in 1.2.22 he asserts the converse, namely that this being is not the individual soul or Prime Matter. In both *sūtras*, his argument is based on reference to qualities or descriptions found in the Upaniṣadic text. Such qualities apparently include all-knowing, all-wise, all-pervasive, and without sin. In 1.2.23, Bādarāyaṇa refers to a description of the cosmic body found in the *Muṇḍaka Upaniṣad* 2:1:4, pointing out that this description, which is apparently meant to refer to the invisible being, could only apply to a being as great as the Brahman.

It is significant that the topical text on which this set of *sūtras* is based is immediately preceded by verses which refer to the existence of two levels of knowledge. In the *Muṇḍaka Upaniṣad* 1:1:4 we read,

> To him then he said: 'There are two knowledges to be known—as indeed the knowers of the Brahman are wont to say: a higher (*para*) and also a lower (*apara*).

If, as Śaṅkara argues, Bādarāyaṇa's frequent references to Difference are based on the lower level of knowledge, would it not be logical for Bādarāyaṇa at some point to declare his acceptance of the doctrine of two levels of knowledge, and would not this be an ideal place for him to do so, since he is dealing with verses closely located to the *Muṇḍaka* passage describing the two levels of knowledge? Bādarāyaṇa's failure to refer to the two levels of truth at this or any other point provides strong evidence that it was not a doctrine that he held.

TOPIC SEVEN: THE GASTRIC FIRE

1.2.24: *Vaiśvānaraḥ sādhāraṇaśabdaviśeṣāt*

The All Man/Gastric Fire (or Vaiśvānara that Scripture speaks of, in passages like: 'Of this All Man/Gastric Fire, the head is indeed the good light, the eye is the universal form, breath is of varied courses, the body is the full, the bladder is wealth, the feet are the earth, etc.,' *Chāndogya Upaniṣad* 5:18:2) is the Brahman, because the word All Man/Vaiśvānara, though common to various kinds of fire and to the

Brahman, especially signifies the Brahman (in Scriptural usage, as is seen by the lines, 'the head indeed is the good light, the eye is the universal form,' qualities peculiar to the Brahman).

1.2.25: *Smaryamāṇamanumānam syāditi*

That the Gastric Fire is the Brahman can be inferred from traditional texts of similar import (like that of the *Viṣṇu Purāṇa* which reads: 'He whose mouth is Fire, whose head the heavenly world, whose navel is the ether, whose feet the earth, whose eye the sun, whose ears the regions, reverence to him, the self of the world').[2]

1.2.26: *Śabdādibhyo'ntaḥpratiṣṭhānācca neti cenna tathādṛṣṭyupadeśādasambhavāt puruṣamapi cainamadhīyate*

'Can it be that the sense of the words in the Scriptural passage, and the assertion of indwelling, refer to an indwelling gastric fire and not to the Brahman?'

No, because (a) the Brahman is described as also indwelling in the stomach; (b) it is impossible that the qualities mentioned in the passage be those of the Gastric Fire (qualities like 'universal form') and (c) because the All Man is described as a person (in addition to gastric fire).

1.2.27: *Ata eva na devatā bhūtam ca*

For the same reason, the All Man/Gastric Fire is neither the deity of fire nor the element of fire.

1.2.28: *Sākṣādapyavirodham Jaiminiḥ*

For Jaimini, there is no contradiction if the All Man is taken to refer directly to the Brahman, without any allusion to Gastric Fire.

1.2.29: *Abhivyakterityāśmarathyaḥ*

For Āśmarathya, the All Man is described as the measure of the span (in the Scriptural passage 'He, however, who meditates on the All Man as of the measure of the span or as identical with the self, eats food in all worlds, in all beings, in all selves,' *Chāndogya Upaniṣad* 5:18:1), because he manifests himself as such.

1.2.30: *Anusmṛterbādariḥ*

For Bādari, 'the measure of the span' description is for evoking the Brahman's recollection.

1.2.31: *Sampatteriti jaiminitathāhi darśayati*

For Jaimini, 'the measure of the span' description is to excite imaginative identification as Scripture itself demonstrates.

1.2.32: *Āmananti cainamasmin*

And they (people like the Vājasaneyins or the Jābālas) mention the Brahman as being within (being like the stomach, the measure of the span, or the body of the worshipper).

Bādarāyaṇa now begins a rather long topical section, consisting of nine *sūtras* which examine a section of the *Chāndogya Upaniṣad* 5:11, in which the All Man/Gastric Fire (*Vaiśvānara*) is discussed at length. The question which Bādarāyaṇa addresses is whether this term refers to the element of fire, the deity Fire, the gastric fire, or, unlikely as it may seem to make such an identification—the Brahman. The problem results from the multiple meanings which can be denoted by *Vaiśvānara*. Monier-Williams, for instance, identifies such diverse meanings as omnipresent, universal, common; a name of Agni; the fire of digestion; and the sun.[3]

In 1.2.24, Bādarāyaṇa declares that *Vaiśānara* refers to the Highest Self or the Brahman, on the basis of the descriptions given to the two words, *Vaiśvānara* and Self. Rāmānuja argues that since in the *Chāndogya* text, the sages who desire knowledge of the Brahman are given a response in which *Vaiśvānara* is described, then the two must be identical. Madhva interprets this *sūtra* as referring to the fact that the word 'Self' (*Ātman*) is used in conjunction with *Vaiśvānara* in a manner which clearly suggests that they are one and the same. Śaṅkara points out that the *Vaiśvānara* is described in the text as having a divine form which could only apply to the Brahman.

Which of these specific interpretations of Bādarāyaṇa's *sūtra* is correct is not important for our purposes: in fact, as usual, Bādarāyaṇa words the *sūtra* in such a sparse manner that many interpretations are possible. The key point, however, is that Bādarāyaṇa does identify the *Vaiśvānara* with the Brahman. That one term could denote such strikingly different realities—the

Supreme Brahman and the gastric fire—may at first glance seem rather shocking, but not if reality is viewed from the perspective of an element of Identity existing between the Brahman and his creation. If the Brahman somehow dwells within everything in the world, then in a sense everything can bear his name since its identity includes him. This, of course, is a convenient doctrine for use by Bādarāyaṇa and the expositors, since it can be used to explain practically *any* Scriptural passage as referring to the Brahman.

Bādarāyaṇa next proceeds to reinforce his point by employing a technique he has used earlier, namely that of referring to a passage in Sacred Tradition that confirms his position. In 1.2.25, he apparently is alluding to *Smṛti* passages that describe the Brahman in terms similar to the topical text's description of the *Vaiśvānara,* thereby proving their identity. The expositors, as usual, disagree as to which specific passages in Sacred Tradition are meant.

In 1.2.26 we find one of the longest of the 555 *sūtras* composed by Bādarāyaṇa. The specific meaning is difficult to ascertain and there is some disagreement among the expositors, but it appears that Bādarāyaṇa here offers three reasons for not identifying the *Vaiśvānara* with the gastric fire:

1. Because we know that, for purposes of meditation, Scripture describes the Brahman as residing in the stomach;
2. Because the gastric fire could not be the object of the Scriptural passages that describe the cosmic body of the *Vaiśvānara;*
3. Because the topical text describes the *Vaiśvānara* as a person.

Having demonstrated that the *Vaiśvānara* cannot refer to the gastric fire, in 1.2.27 Bādarāyaṇa argues that for these same reasons *Vaiśvānara* cannot refer to the element of fire or the fire god, Agni. It should be noted that Madhva, Śaṅkara and Rāmānuja exhibit unusual agreement on the first four *sūtras* of this section.

In the next five *sūtras*, Bādarāyaṇa employs a new methodology, namely that of supporting his position by reference to other non-Scriptural authorities, those being Jaimini, Āśmarathya, Bādari, and the Jābālas or Vājasaneyins.

In 1.2.28, we find the opinion of Jaimini that even if *Vaiśvānara* refers to the Brahman in a direct rather than figurative sense, this is acceptable.

The opinion of Āśmarathya is referred to in 1.2.29, where, according to Rāmānuja and Śaṅkara, the subject shifts to another section of the same topical text in which the *Vaiśvānara* is described as being 'the measure of a span.' The question raised is how can the omnipresent Brahman be described as limited in size? Āśmarathya responds that the Brahman manifests himself in such limited forms for the purpose of making himself more accessible to his devotees.

According to Śaṅkara 1.2.30 offers Bādari's response to this same question, his response being that such a limited manifestation makes it easier for devotees to remember him. Rāmānuja sees this *sūtra* as answering a different question, that being why does the text also describe the Brahman as having a head, limbs, etc. The answer, according to Rāmānuja, is the same as that given by Śaṅkara: for the purpose of easy remembrance.

According to Rāmānuja, 1.2.31 responds to the question of why the parts of the sacrifice are identified with the cosmic body of *Vaiśvānara*, the answer given by Jaimini being that it is for the purpose of more easily remembering the Brahman during the sacrifice. Śaṅkara, on the other hand, sees this *sūtra* as providing another explanation of the passage which describes *Vaiśvānara* as the measure of a span.

Finally, Bādarāyaṇa closes with 1.2.32, another ambiguous *sūtra* which literally means, 'And they mention him in that.' Rāmānuja claims that this refers to the Vājasaneyins who also state that the Brahman resides in the stomach, while Śaṅkara argues that it is a reference to the Jābālas who declare that the Brahman is the measure of a span.

Madhva offers an interesting alternative interpretation of these last five *sūtras*, arguing that they represent a defense of the doctrine of *samanvaya*. Fortunately, in this case it is not necessary to determine which of the expositors' interpretations is correct, since our goal is to identify Bādarāyaṇa's own theology, and all interpretations agree on the fundamental point that Bādarāyaṇa identifies the *Vaiśvānara* as the Brahman.

With reference to Bādarāyaṇa's theology, this section provides further support for our position that Bādarāyaṇa advocates a type of Difference-In-Identity. Identity, in terms of immanence, is seen through the symbolic identification of the Brahman with the gastric fire, an identification that portrays the Brahman as residing within the person. At the same time, however, Difference is asserted through Bādarāyaṇa's declaration that the topical text refers to the Brahman and *not* to the gastric fire on the grounds that qualities found in the text can only apply to the Brahman. Thus, we can conclude from this section that Bādarāyaṇa sees the Brahman as residing within its creation, which is a separate and distinct, though intimately related entity.

FOOTNOTES

1. B.N.K. Sharma, *The Brahma Sūtras,* 1:152–161.
2. Quoted by S. Radhakrishnan, *The Brahma Sūtras*, p. 283.
3. Monier Monier-Williams, *A Sanskrit-English Dictionary* (Delhi: Motilal Banarsidass, 1989), p. 1027.

CHAPTER VI

An Analysis of the *Brahma Sūtras* 1:3

TOPIC ONE: THE SUPPORT OF THE UNIVERSE

1.3.1: *Dyubhvādyāyatanam svaśabdāt*

The support of the sky, the earth and the other things of which Scripture speaks is the Brahman, because its (the Brahman's) very own word (the 'Self', is used to describe this support, in the passage which reads: 'He on whom the sky, the earth, and the atmosphere are woven, and the minds, together with all the life-breaths, Him alone know as the one Self: other words dismiss.' *Muṇḍaka Upaniṣad* 2:5).

1.3.2: *Muktopasṛpya vyapadeśāt*

And because Scripture describes it as that which can be attained by the released (in words immediately consequent on those quoted above: 'He is the bridge to immortality').

1.3.3: *Nānumānam atacchabdāt*

This support cannot be that known by inference (Prime Matter itself), because the words of that Scriptural passage do not indicate it (or have no reference at all to Prime Matter).

1.3.4: *Prāṇabhṛc ca*

Nor can it be the bearer of breath (i.e., the individual soul).

1.3.5: *Bhedavyapadeśāc ca*

The support is not the individual soul, because of the mention of difference (between it and the Brahman, as in Scriptural passage like: 'When he (the suffering individual soul) sees the other, the Lord who is worshipped and His greatness, he becomes freed from sorrow.' *Muṇḍaka Upaniṣad* 3:1:2).

1.3.6: *Prakaraṇāt*

And the individual soul cannot be meant since the topic of the passage referred to is the Brahman.

1.3.7: *Stithyadanābhyām ca*

The individual soul cannot be meant, because Scripture speaks of two beings, one (the soul) just perching and the other (the Brahman) eating (in the words: 'Two birds, constant companions, perch on the same tree. One of them eats the sweet fig. The other does not eat, but looks on.' *Muṇḍaka Upaniṣad* 3:1:1).

Bādarāyaṇa now begins the third section of the first chapter of the *Brahma Sūtras*. According to Madhva, this section examines words and phrases that can denote both the Brahman and other objects in the world. Rāmānuja views this section as an investigation of passages which appear to clearly refer to the individual soul, while Śaṅkara considers it an extension of the second section.

For the first topic, which consists of seven verses, Bādarāyaṇa draws his topical text from the *Muṇḍaka Upaniṣad* 2:5:

'He on whom the sky, the earth, and the atmosphere
Are woven, and the mind, together with all the life-breaths,
Him alone know as the one Self (*Ātman*).
Other words dismiss. He is the bridge to immortality.

In 1.3.1, Bādarāyaṇa appears to assert that the being referred to in this passage must be the Brahman, because of the reference to a word that could only be its own, that being *Ātman*, or 'Self'. In 1.3.2, further proof of the identity of this being with the Brahman is offered on the grounds that it is described as the goal which is attained by released souls—a description which, of course, could apply only to the Brahman. It should be noted that Bādarāyaṇa uses this line of reasoning on several occasions in the *Brahma Sūtras*.

Having established that the passage clearly refers to attributes that are characteristic of the Brahman, Bādarāyaṇa now demonstrates how the passage cannot refer to other realities. In 1.3.3, Prime Matter (referred to as *anumānam*, or that which is known by inference) is rejected as the topic of the text on the grounds that descriptions found in the passage cannot refer to it. Once again, Bādarāyaṇa does not include these descriptions in the *sūtra*, but in the text we read that this being perceives all and knows all, activities which cannot be engaged in by the unconscious Prime Matter.

In the next *sūtra*, 1.3.4, Bādarāyaṇa apparently states that the individual soul, referred to here as the 'bearer of breath', cannot be the being who is the support of heaven, earth, etc. Most expositors treat this as a separate *sūtra*, posing a problem since the *sūtra* lists a topic (*prāṇabhṛt* is in the nominative case) but nothing else, in contrast to Bādarāyaṇa's usual practice of including in each *sūtra* a reason, found in the ablative case, for identifying or rejecting the subject in question as referring to the Brahman. Hence, we are inclined to concur with Rāmānuja who combines *prāṇabhṛc ca* with *sūtra* 1.3.3, thereby making the ablative *śabdāt* refer to both *anumānam* and *prāṇabhṛt*, the meaning being that neither Prime Matter nor the individual soul can be the topic of the section since words found in the passages cannot refer to either entity.

In 1.3.5, Bādarāyaṇa uses the word *bheda* (difference) for the second time in the *Brahma Sūtras*. In this *sūtra*, he offers further confirmation of his position that the support of heaven, earth, etc., is the Brahman on the grounds that later in the *Muṇḍaka Upaniṣad*, the Brahman is still the topic, and indeed, the Brahman is depicted as different and separate from the individual soul. The specific passage referred to, according to Madhva and Rāmānuja, is *Muṇḍaka Upaniṣad* 3.1.2: 'When he sees the other, the Lord who is worshippped and his greatness, he becomes freed from sorrow.'

Bādarāyaṇa employs one of his standard methods of proof in 1.3.6, by pointing out that since the topic of the entire section of the *Muṇḍaka Upaniṣad* under consideration refers to the Brahman, then it follows that the reference to the being who supports heaven, earth, etc., also must be to the Brahman.

As a final demonstration of the *Muṇḍaka Upaniṣad's* description of the Brahman and the individual soul as different, in 1.3.7 Bādarāyaṇa refers to *Muṇḍaka Upaniṣad* 3.1.2:

Two birds, constant companions,
Perch on the same tree.
One of them eats the sweet Fig.
The other does not eat, but looks on.

This passage traditionally has been interpreted as referring to the active individual soul which is involved in karmic activity, and the Highest Self which dwells within the person but remains aloof from and unaffected by the person's actions.

In looking at the theology expressed in this topic, we see a very strong emphasis on the element of Difference. In 1.3.3, Bādarāyaṇa asserts that the Prime Matter is different from the Brahman, while in 1.3.4, 5 and 7, he asserts the same about the individual soul. Given this strong focus on Difference, this section represents somewhat of a shift in emphasis from section 1.2, where the element of immanence appeared to be rather prominent. Even in the first *sūtra* of the section, by identifying the Brahman as the support of heaven and earth, Bādarāyaṇa is thereby asserting that the Brahman is in some sense separate and distinct from his creation since the concept of supporting only makes sense if there is a supporter and an object supported.

This topical section also offers an interesting example of Bādarāyaṇa's methodology, in that he employs techniques that are found at many places in the *Brahma Sūtras*. He begins the section in 1.3.1 by identifying the Brahman as the subject of the text under consideration, doing so by use of what is perhaps his favorite technique of referring to a word in the passage that could only apply to the Brahman. In 1.3.2, he establishes his point through the technique of referring to a commonly accepted truth, in this case the truth that only the Brahman is the object of release. Having shown that some words in the text clearly apply to the Brahman, he then moves to another frequently used technique, that of demonstrating that other words in the text clearly cannot refer to Prime Matter or the individual soul. This technique is used in 1.3.4, 5 and 7. In 1.3.6, Bādarāyaṇa employs yet another of his favorite techniques, that of proof through reference to the general topic of the text. Thus, in this section we see four techniques that Bādarāyaṇa employs throughout the *Brahma Sūtras*.[1]

TOPIC TWO: THE ABUNDANCE

1.3.8: *Bhūmā samprasādād adhyupadeśāt*

The Abundance (or the infinite) of which Scripture speaks is the Brahman (and not the breath, or the soul associated with that breath), because of its reference to bliss (in passages like: 'The infinite is happiness. There is no happiness in anything small. Only the infinite is happiness.' *Chāndogya Upaniṣad* 7:23), and because of its teaching of excess or ultimacy in the experience of the Brahman, (as in the very next passage: 'When one sees nothing else, hears nothing else, understands nothing else, that is the infinite.' *Chāndogya Upaniṣad* 7:24).

1.3.9: *Dharmopapatteś ca*

And because the qualities associated with the Abundance in the passages referred to only apply to the Brahman.

This brief section examines a passage in the *Chāndogya Upaniṣad* which refers to the '*bhūman*', a word that can mean earth, world, territory, abundance, wealth, and, as appears to be applicable in this case, 'the aggregate of all existing things.'[2] For purposes of brevity, we shall translate *bhūman* as 'the Abundance', meaning the totality of all that exists.

The topical text is found in the *Chāndogya Upaniṣad* 7:24:

> Where one sees nothing else, hears nothing else, understands nothing else—that is the Abundance. But where one sees something else—that is the small. Verily, the Abundance is the same as the immortal; but the small is the same as the mortal.

While it seems to be clear that in this section Bādarāyaṇa identifies the Abundance as the Brahman, the specific reasons that he offers for establishing this point are not clear in *sūtra* 1.3.8. In this *sūtra* we find two ablatives, *samprasādāt* and *adhyupadeśāt*. According to Rāmānuja and Śaṅkara, they refer to one reason, namely that the teaching about the Abundance comes after the teaching about the serene one, or the individual soul. More specifically, they argue that the preceding passages in the seventh chapter of the *Chāndogya Upaniṣad* describe a series of realities, each higher than the other. If the Abundance referred to the individual soul, then it should appear in the section on the individual soul, when in reality it *follows* it. The term *samprasādāt* is used to refer to the individual soul as it exists in the serenity of deep sleep.

Madhva, however, o fers an obvious objection to this reasoning, claiming that the mere fact that the teaching on the Abundance follows the teaching on the individual soul does not prove that therefore the Abundance refers to the Brahman. Instead, Madhva sees the two ablatives as presenting two different reasons for identifying the Abundance with the Brahman. First, *samprasādāt* refers to the passage that declares the Abundance to have infinite bliss, a quality that only applies to the Brahman; and secondly, *adhyupadeśāt* refers to the structure of the teaching, namely that after teaching about several different elements, each higher than the last, there is no teaching after the one on the Abundance, implying that it is the highest being, or the Brahman.

Which of these interpretations reflects Bādarāyaṇa's intent is difficult to say, since both have their weaknesses—Rāmānuja's and Śaṅkara's already alluded to by Madhva, and Madhva's weakness seen in his dubious interpretation of *samprasādāt* as referring to the infinite bliss of the Brahman. Since, however, it is not our purpose to decide which expositor presents the strongest case, but rather to find Bādarāyaṇa's own theology, independent of the sectarian biases of the expositors, the ambiguity over the precise meaning of this *sūtra* is not important. What is important is simply that Bādarāyaṇa clearly identifies the Abundance with the Brahman, even though his reasons for doing so are vague.

The section closes with a much clearer *sūtra*, in which Bādarāyaṇa reaffirms that the Abundance refers to the Brahman, this time on the grounds that the qualities listed in the text only apply to the Brahman. In the text we find such qualities as immortal, resting on its own greatness, the Self of all, and producing all.

With reference to Bādarāyaṇa's theology, this short section offers something of a paradox. On the one hand, Bādarāyaṇa asserts that the Brahman is the *bhūman*, thereby suggesting an omnipresent being and some element of Identity. On the other hand, he declares that the *bhūman* does *not* refer to the individual soul, thereby suggesting an element of Difference. This is actually consistent with our overall analysis of the *Brahma Sūtras*, where sections that emphasize Difference stand side by side with sections emphasizing Identity. What we are still looking for is Bādarāyaṇa's explanation of how these two apparent opposites can exist in some type of relationship with each other.

TOPIC THREE: THE IMPERISHABLE

1.3.10: *Akṣaram ambarāntadhṛteḥ*

The Imperishable that Scripture speaks of (in the *Bṛhadāraṇyaka Upaniṣad* 3:8: 'That which is above the sky, that which is beneath the earth, that which is between these two, sky and earth, that which the people call the past, the present and the future, across space is that woven like warp and woof... that, O Gārgī, the knowers of the Brahman call the Imperishable') is the Brahman because it supports all things from first to last, up to space itself (as the Scriptural text clearly demonstrates).

1.3.11: *Sā ca praśāsanāt*

And this Imperishable must be the Brahman because of the reference to its command (in the text following the above: 'Verily, at the command of that Imperishable, O Gārgī, the sun and moon stand in their respective positions').

1.3.12: *Anyabhāvavyāvṛtteś ca*

And this Imperishable is the Brahman because everything different in nature from it is excluded (in a further passage of the same chapter: 'That Imperishable, O Gārgī, is unseen but is the seer, is unheard but is the hearer, unthought, but is the thinker, unknown but is the knower. There is no other seer but this, there is no other hearer but this, there is no other thinker but this, there is no other knower but this.'

Moving to the next topical text, we read in the *Bṛhadāraṇyaka Upaniṣad* 3:8:7 to 8 that the pupil Gārgī asks the venerable teacher Yājñavalkya to declare upon what space is woven, to which he replies:

> That, O Gārgī, the Brahmans call the Imperishable (*akṣara*). It is not coarse, not fine, not short, not long,... odourless, tasteless, without eye, without ear... unaging, undying, without fear, immortal.

Bādarāyaṇa begins the section by asserting in 1.3.10 that the Imperishable is the Brahman, since it is defined as supporting all things—a quality belonging only to the Brahman. In 1.3.11, Bādarāyaṇa reinforces his position by appealing to another verse (*Bṛhadāraṇyaka Upaniṣad* 3:8:9) in which the Imperishable commands various cosmic events to occur, such as the sun and moon standing apart. Clearly this could not refer to the individual soul which lacks such powers, nor could it refer to the impersonal Prime Matter which is not capable of issuing commands. Finally, 1.3.12 further confirms the identity of the Brahman and the Imperishable on the basis of the description of the Imperishable found in *Bṛhadāraṇyaka Upaniṣad* 3:8:11, where it is referred to as the unseen Seer, the unheard Hearer, etc., and where we also read: 'Other than it, there is nothing that sees, hears, thinks, or understands.'

With reference to Bādarāyaṇa's theology, 1.3.10 resembles 1.3.1 in the sense of insinuating Difference through identifying a supporter and an object of support. Likewise, 1.3.11 also insinuates Difference by identifying the being who commands and the world which is the object of his command. This verse also is significant in that by attributing the act of commanding to the Brahman, it suggests a *theistic* interpretation of God, a personal God who issues commands to his creation.

TOPIC FOUR: THE OBJECT OF SEEING

1.3.13: *Īkṣatikarmavyapadeśāt saḥ*

The persoṅ (referred to as an object of meditation in Scriptural passges like *Praśṇa Upaniṣad* 5:5) is the Brahman, because He is described as the object of seeing (*īkṣati*). (The passage reads: 'If he meditates on the highest person with the three elements of the syllable *Aum* (a, u, m) he becomes one with the light, the sun... He sees (*īkṣate*) the person that dwells in the body').

Here we find an unusual situation where a topical section consists of only one aphorism, the meaning of which is somewhat unclear. While the wording of the *sūtra* makes translation easy, the specific subject to which the *sūtra* refers is not clear. Rāmānuja and Śaṅkara identify the same topical text (*Praśṇa Upaniṣad* 5:5) but differ on the *sūtra's* subject: Śaṅkara claiming that the *sūtra* establishes that the higher rather than the lower Brahman is referred to, while Rāmānuja believes that the *sūtra* indicates that the topical text refers to the Brahman, not to Brahmā, the creator-deity. Madhva takes an entirely different approach, identifying the topical text as several passages which describe creation as originating in *Sat* (Being). This *sūtra*, according to Madhva, proves that *Sat* refers to the Brahman rather than Prime Matter. Given the absence of a clearly indicated topic within the *sūtra* itself, any of these interpretations is feasible, although Śaṅkara's is less convincing since the doctrine of the two Brahmans is not stated by Bādarāyaṇa himself anywhere in the *Brahma Sūtras*. Given this uncertainty as to the true meaning of the *sūtra*, we cannot draw any conclusions regarding Bādarāyaṇa's theology.

TOPIC FIVE: THE SMALL SPACE IN THE HEART

1.3.14: *Dahara uttarebhyaḥ*

The small space within the heart (referred to by Scripture in the text: 'Now, here in the city of Brahman is an abode, a small lotus flower; within it is a small space') is the Brahman (and not the soul), because the subsequent words (in the same text attribute to it the all-inclusive immensity exclusive to the Brahman alone: 'within it, indeed, are contained both heaven and earth, both fire and air, both sun and moon, lightning and stars. Whatever there is of him in this world and whatever is not, all that is contained within it.' *Chāndogya Upaniṣad* 8:1:1–4).

1.3.15: *Gatiśabdābhyāmtathā hi dṛṣṭam liṅgam ca*

(The Scriptural text: 'all creatures here go day after day into the Brahman world', *Chāndogya Upaniṣad* 8:3:2) signifies that the small space is the Brahman, by its reference to 'going into' ('all creatures... go... into') and its use of the word for the soul ('creatures'). In that text too the connection between the soul and the Brahman is noticed (in the phrase, 'The Brahman world').

1.3.16: *Dhṛteś ca mahimno'syāsminn upalabdheḥ*

The small space is the Brahman, because it is described as the 'support' ('for keeping the worlds apart' in Scripture's words, *Chāndogya Upaniṣad* 8:4:1) and because it is observed to possess greatness (as Scripture says elsewhere in the passage which begins with the words: 'Verily, at the command of that Imperishable, O Gārgī, the sun and the moon stand in their respective positions.' *Bṛhadāraṇyaka Upaniṣad* 3:8:9).

1.3.17: *Prasiddheś ca*

And because space as such is accepted as meaning the Brahman (as in the Scriptural text: 'All these creatures are produced from space. They return back into space. For space is greater than these. Space is the final goal'. *Chāndogya Upaniṣad* 1:9:1).

1.3.18: *Itaraparāmarśāt sa iti cen nāsambhavāt*

'Can it be that Scripture is speaking about the soul when it mentions another being ('rising out of this body and reaching the higher light'. *Chāndogya Upaniṣad* 8:3:4)?'

No, because the attributes Scripture ascribes to this being cannot be those of the soul (but of the Brahman, who alone is 'Free from sin, free from old age, free from death'. *Chāndogya Upaniṣad* 8:1:5).

1.3.19: *Uttarāc ced āvirbhūtasvarūpas tu*

'Can it be said that the small space is the soul because it is to the soul that the verses initially describing the small space make reference?'

Those verses refer to its manifested form (as the soul, and not to its primordial form, as the Brahman).

1.3.20: *Anyārthaś ca parāmarśaḥ*

The reference to the individual soul thus has a different meaning.

1.3.21: *Alpaśruter iti cet tad uktam*

'Can the reference be to the soul because Scripture speaks of something small?'

The problem of smallness had already been addressed above (in 1.2.7).

1.3.22: *Anukṛtes tasya ca*

The small space is the Brahman and the soul both, because the soul imitates the Brahman (in Scripture's words: 'All shines in imitation of His shining. All that exists shines in His sheen.' *Śvetāśvatara Upaniṣad* 6:14).

1.3.23: *Api ca smaryate*

This teaching also is found in Sacred Tradition (in the *Gītā*'s words: 'The brilliance which shines in the sun, in the moon and in fire, illuminates the entire universe. Know that brilliance to be mine.'

Bhagavad Gītā 15:12).

We find the topical text for the next section in *Chāndogya Upaniṣad* 8:1:1:

> Now, what is here in this city of the Brahman is an abode, a small lotus flower. Within that is a small space. What is within that should be searched out; that, assuredly, is what one should desire to understand.

The question posed by this section is the identity of that which resides in the small space in the heart. In the first four *sūtras* of this section, Bādarāyaṇa responds to the argument that the reference is to the element of space; in the last four *sūtras* he addresses the argument that the reference is to the individual soul.

In 1.3.14, Bādarāyaṇa begins the section by stating that the small space must be the Brahman because of what is said about it in passages subsequent to the topical text. Presumably, Bādarāyaṇa is referring to passages such as *Chāndogya Upaniṣad* 8:1:4, where the space within the heart is described as ageless, free from evil, deathless, sorrowless, etc., In 1.3.15, Bādarāyaṇa offers further evidence that the reference is to the Brahman, namely the mention of souls 'going into' the small space, and the association of the word 'Brahman world' with the small space. Bādarāyaṇa borrows an argument from two earlier *sūtras*, 1.3.1 and 1.3.10, when in 1.3.16 he argues that the small space must refer to the Brahman since the attribute of supporting the world is assigned to it, an attribute which belongs only to the Brahman. Another technique of proof—though perhaps of dubious merit—is used by Bādarāyaṇa in 1.3.17, that being the technique of proof through reference to settled opinion: the small space refers to the Brahman because it is generally understood as such.

According to the expositors, Bādarāyaṇa now shifts his focus from the small space to the individual soul. While Bādarāyaṇa himself does not identify such a shift with his own words, it appears to be a logical explanation of the structure of the section, and is agreed upon by the expositors.

Sūtra 1.3.18 points out that the reference cannot be to individual soul since the attributes associated with the small space do not apply to the individual soul. A more compelling argument in favour of identifying the small space with the individual soul is found in 1.3.19, which remarks that in the section of the *Upaniṣad* following the section on the small space, the individual soul clearly is the topic and is described in terms similar to those applied to the small space. Bādarāyaṇa's response is that the description of the individual soul is with reference to when its true nature is manifested; hence, the similarity to descriptions of the Brahman. Śaṅkara takes this opportunity to remind us that in reality, of course, there is no individual soul, even though, for purposes of discourse at the lower level of knowledge, Bādarāyaṇa speaks of it. As Ghate points out, even Śaṅkara is compelled to acknowledge Bādarāyaṇa's frequent assertions about the *difference* between the Brahman and the individual soul, although he (Śaṅkara) explains away these assertions through inserting his own doctrine of the two levels of truth.[3]

In 1.3.20, Bādarāyaṇa appears to assert that a passage that seems to describe the qualities of the individual soul actually describes the qualities of the Brahman. *Sūtra* 1.3.21 refers back to an earlier *sūtra* (1.2.7) which answered the objection that the Brahman could not be described as dwelling in a small space.

Śaṅkara and Madhva begin a new *adhikaraṇa* with *sūtra* 1.3.22. However, we are inclined to accept Rāmānuja's position that this and the next *sūtra* are a continuation of the section on the small space, due in part to the presence of the word *ca* (and) in 1.3.22, suggesting a continuation from the previous *sūtra*. Following Rāmānuja's interpretation, we see that 1.3.22 asserts that the similar descriptions of the individual soul and the Brahman derive from the fact that the individual soul 'imitates', or has a nature similar to the Brahman. Finally, the section closes with 1.3.23, which appeals to Sacred Tradition to confirm the similarity of the Brahman and the individual soul.

Taken as a whole, this section reveals that Bādarāyaṇa perceives the Brahman as immanent in his creation, since the entire section is based on the idea that the Brahman dwells in the small space in the heart. At the same time, however, by asserting that the space in the heart is not the individual soul or the element ether, Bādarāyaṇa presents a theological interpretation of immanence in which there is a clear difference between the being whose immanence is declared and those beings in which it is immanent. All of this fits in well with the topical text that we referred to earlier in examining the topic of the Inner Controller[4], which describes the Brahman as 'dwelling in' but 'other than' its creation. Thus, once again we find Bādarāyaṇa presenting a theology of both Identity and Difference, without clarifying how the two are related to each other.

It also should be noted that in this section Bādarāyaṇa refers to the Brahman's role of supporting the world for the third time. His frequent reference to this quality suggests that he considers it a very important aspect of the Brahman, an aspect which was included in his very first definition of the Brahman, in 1.1.2, where the Brahman is defined as the 'creator, etc.', which means creator, supporter, and destroyer of the world.

TOPIC SIX: THE PERSON OF THE SIZE OF A THUMB

1.3.24: *Śabdād eva pramitaḥ*

The person described in Scripture as measured by the size of the thumb (in the words: 'the person of the size of the thumb resides in the middle of the body. After knowing him who is the lord of the past and the future, one does not shrink.' *Kaṭha Upaniṣad* 4:12) is the Brahman and not the soul, because the word (of Scripture referring to that person, qualifies him with the Brahman's attributes in the words 'lord of the past and the future').

1.3.25: *Hṛdyapekṣayā tu manuṣyādhikāratvāt*

(In other passages on the thumb-sized person like 'The person of the size of the thumb, the Inner Self, abides always in the heart of man', *Kaṭha Upaniṣad* 6:17). Scripture alludes to the human heart (which encloses a thumb-sized space) to indicate that man has the privilege of studying the Scripture (and thus finally attaining release).

Bādarāyaṇa continues his examination of texts which refer to the Brahman's immanence, looking next at the *Kaṭha Upaniṣad* text quoted above in *sūtra* 1.3.24. In 1.3.24, Bādarāyaṇa claims that the person the size of a thumb must be the Brahman, since it is described by the world 'Lord'. In 1.3.25, Bādarāyaṇa answers the somewhat silly objection that, since other passages state that the Brahman resides in the heart, then his size must vary in accordance with the different sizes of hearts of various animals. The response to this argument is that since the Scriptures only are read by man, then it must be man's heart to which Scriptures refer. Rāmānuja offers another perspective on this *sūtra*, arguing that since only man can attain release, the fact that animals have thumb-sized enclosures in their hearts does not mean that they too can study the Scriptures. Rather, the thumb-sized person dwells only in the heart of the being with a thumb-sized enclosure who is capable of liberation.

Having established that man can study the Vedas, Bādarāyaṇa now proceeds to examine whether or not the gods can study the Vedas also.

TOPIC SEVEN: THE DEITIES AS STUDENTS OF THE VEDAS

1.3.26: *Tadupary api Bādarāyaṇaḥ sambhavāt*

According to Bādarāyaṇa, those from above (i.e., the gods) can study the Vedas also, since it is possible for them to have the desire for release.

1.3.27: *Virodhaḥ karmaṇīti cen*
nānekapratipatter darśanāt

'Would not the possession of bodies by the gods result in a contradiction to sacrificial works?'

No, because it is perceived that gods can assume many bodies simultaneously.

1.3.28: *Śabda iti cen nātaḥ prabhavāt*
pratyakṣānumānābhyām

'Would there not occur a contradiction with regard to the eternal nature of Vedic words?'

No, because beings arise from these words, as is known from what is based on perception and what is based on inference.

1.3.29: *Ata eva ca nityatvam*

And hence for the same reason, the eternal nature of the Vedas is established.

1.3.30: *Samānanāmarūpatvāc cāvṛttāv apy*
avirodho darśanāt smṛteś ca

And because of similarity of name and form in the repetition of creations, there is no contradiction to the eternal nature of the Vedic words, as is known from what is observed and from Sacred Tradition.

1.3.31: *Madhvādiṣv asambhavād anadhikāram Jaiminiḥ*

Jaimini claims that the gods cannot seek the Brahman, as they lack meditations like the Honey knowledge (described by Scripture in the words 'Yonder sun is the honey of the gods.' *Chāndogya Upaniṣad* 3:1:1. The gods who live on this honey are the objects of meditation and not the meditations themselves).

1.3.32: *Jyotiṣi bhāvāc ca*

And because they have a nature like that of light (which is bodiless), they cannot seek the Brahman (as only embodied beings can).

1.3.33: *Bhāvam tu Bādarāyaṇo'sti hi*

Still Bādarāyaṇa affirms the gods' ability to seek the Brahman, for it is possible. (They can meditate, for instance, on the Brahman controlling them from within.)

Bādarāyaṇa now makes an unusual departure from the normal structure of the *Brahma Sūtras*, in that he starts a new topical section based solely on a question raised by the previous section, and *not* based on a topical text from Scripture. This also is an unusual section in that it is the first section of the *Brahma Sūtras* which does not have as its subject the nature of the Brahman; instead, this group of *sūtras* addresses the subject of whether or not the gods are qualified to seek and attain the Brahman. Rather than talking about the Brahman, Bādarāyaṇa shifts focus and talks about the gods. The entire section seems to be rather out of place in the context of the rest of the *Brahma Sūtras*, and if not for the fact that all of the expositors include it, we would be inclined to suspect that this section is not part of Bādarāyaṇa's work but rather represents a later addition.

As we have seen above in 1.3.25, Bādarāyaṇa states that the privilege of studying the Vedas belongs to man, alone, and not to other creatures. A question which logically follows from this position is whether or not the gods, or celestial beings, have the privilege of seeking the Brahman through study of the Vedas. Bādarāyaṇa answers in the affirmative in 1.3.26, on the grounds that gods have a desire for release just as men do. But in 1.3.27 an objection is raised: if gods are individual beings who possess bodies and hence are capable of studying the Vedas and performing its injunctions, then how could the doctrine of sacrifice be valid, since the god is supposed to be present at a sacrifice, but could not do so if sacrifices would be performed simultaneously in different places? In other words, possession of a body would limit the god's ability to be present at sacrifices. Bādarāyaṇa responds that it is seen in Scripture that the gods have the capacity to assume many bodies at the same time, hence enabling them to be present at sacrifices simultaneously performed in different places.

In 1.3.28, another objection is raised on the basis of the doctrine that there is an eternal connection between a Vedic word and the reality which it designates. If the gods are embodied, and therefore subject to perishing during the periodic dissolutions of the world, then the eternal connection between the Vedic word referring to the god (i.e., its name) and the god's being would be broken. In a somewhat unclear *sūtra*, Bādarāyaṇa responds that this is not the case since the individual embodied gods that exist in any particular aeon are only manifestations of the *class* of that deity. The individual embodied being passes away at the time of dissolution, but the class exists eternally. Since it is the class to which the Vedic name refers, the connection is never broken. According to Bādarāyaṇa, this is known from both Revelation and Sacred Tradition. It sould be noted that this interpretation of the *sūtra* derives largely from the expositors, and could not be made on the basis of the words of the *sūtra* alone.

In 1.3.29, Bādarāyaṇa appears to assert that for the same reason, the eternity of the Vedas is established. Rāmānuja interprets this to mean that, even though the individual sages who utter the Vedas perish, their class of being persists, and is capable of reproducing the Vedas in each epoch.

Sūtra 1.3.30 reaffirms that, in spite of the periodic dissolutions of creation, the Brahman is capable of maintaining the connection between a particular name and a particular form throughout all creations.

A further objection to the idea that the gods can seek the Brahman is raised in 1.3.31. Reference is made to the 'honey doctrine' of the third chapter of the *Chādnogya Upaniṣad*, where seekers of the Brahman are told to meditate on the sun as honey, which is eaten by the gods. The objection, attributed here to Jaimini, is that gods cannot meditate on themselves, and therefore cannot follow the

Vedic injunctions. A further objection is added in 1.3.32, namely that since gods are described as having the nature of light, which is impersonal, they are therefore incapable of carrying out the actions required by the Vedas.

Bādarāyaṇa responds to these positions in 1.3.33, asserting that gods are indeed qualified to seek and attain the Brahman. Unfortunately, his reasons for taking this stance are not included in the *sūtra*. Śaṅkara suggests that Bādarāyaṇa bases his position on Scriptural passages that indicate that the gods can seek the Brahman. Rāmānuja suggests that gods meditate not on themselves, but on the Brahman who resides within them.

This section reveals little about Bādarāyaṇa's own theology, other than that he believes that the gods are eligible for seeking the Brahman. In addition, however, we can infer from the discussion about who is qualified to seek the Brahman that difference exists between the devotee and the object of devotion, since, unless they were in some sense distinct from each other, the concept of seeking would be meaningless. Śaṅkara as usual, can argue that this distinction is only valid at the lower level of truth, but this raises the question of why Bādarāyaṇa would write an entire section, consisting of eight verses, at a level of truth that ultimately is invalid, without *stating* that such is the case—that his words only are true in a limited sense. In other words, given the absence of any assertion to the contrary, is it not logical to assume that Bādarāyaṇa means what he says, in a literal and unqualified way?

TOPIC EIGHT: THE ŚŪDRAS' INELIGIBILITY FOR BRAHMAN KNOWLEDGE

1.3.34 *Śugasya tadanādaraśravaṇāt*
tad ādravaṇāt sūcyate hi

(*Śūdras* cannot study the Vedas, and what Scripture says about Jānaśruti in *Chāndogya Upaniṣad* 4:1ff. cannot be adduced to prove otherwise. Scripture there describes two geese speaking about Jānaśruti: The first goose says, "The light of Jānaśruti has spread like the sky. Do not touch it, lest in burn you.' At which the second goose replies: 'Who is this man of whom you speak, as if he were Raikva?' These disrespectful words grieve Jānaśruti, and make him seek Raikva to find out what he was. When they meet Raikva calls him a *śūdra*, but uses the word in the sense of 'grief' and not of 'a caste'). The words of Scripture only indicate the grief that Jānaśruti felt when he heard the disrespectful words about himself and his running to Raikva (and not that Jānaśruti belonged to the *śūdra* caste).

1.3.35: *Kṣatriyatvagateś cottaratra*
Caitrarathena liṅgāt

And it is known that Jānaśruti was a member of the warrior class from the subsequent indication of his association with Caitraratha (as seen in *Chāndogya Upaniṣad* 4:3:5, where Jānaśruti is mentioned alongside Caitraratha, another member of the warrior (*kṣatriya*) class).

1.3.36: *Saṅskāraparāmarśāt tadabhāvābhilāpāc ca*

That *Śudras* are not qualified for study of the Vedas is seen from the reference to purification ceremonies for the higher castes and the absence of such a reference with regard to the *Śūdras* (in Scriptural texts like *Śatapatha Brāhmaṇa* 11:5:3:13).

1.3.37: *Tad abhāvanirdhāraṇe ca pravṛtteḥ*

This is also seen from Gautama's proceeding to initiate Jābāla only after ascertaining that he was not a *sūdra* (as is seen in *Chāndogya Upaniṣad* 4:4:5, where Gautama questions Gautama and concludes, 'A non-Brahmin would not be able to explain thus', and then proceeds to teach him.)

1.3.38: *Śravaṇādhyayanārthapratiṣedhāt smṛteś ca*

And because in Sacred Tradition (like *Manu Smṛti* 4:80) the *śūdras* are forbidden from hearing, studying and acting on the Vedas.

Bādarāyaṇa continues and concludes the discussion on who is qualified to seek the Brahman with a section on the *śūdras*, the lowest Hindu caste. The topical text is taken from the *Chāndogya Upaniṣad* 4:2, where Jānaśruti asks Raikva to teach him about the Brahman, which he does. In the text, Raikva refers to Jānaśruti as 'O *śūdra*', suggesting that Jānaśruti was a member of this class, and implying that the *śūdras* are qualified to learn about the Brahman. In 1.3.34, Bādarāyaṇa rejects this position on the grounds that in the Scriptural text the word *śūdra* refers to Jānaśruti's grief, not his caste. The grief was caused by a bird who taunted him about his ignorance. *Ṣūtra*

1.3.35 proves that Jānaśruti was a member of the warrior caste, as seen by his association with another member of the same caste, Caitraratha. In 1.3.36, Bādarāyaṇa asserts that *śūdras* are not qualified for the study of the Vedas since the purification ceremony is mentioned only with reference to the three higher castes. Further proof is given in 1.3.37, which refers to the *Chāndogya Upaniṣad* 4:4:5, where Gautama proceeds to instruct Jābāla only after determining that he is not a *śūdra*. Finally, 1.3.38 points out that Sacred Tradition also declares that the *śūdras* cannot hear, study, or follow the Vedas.

This section provides little insight into the theology of Bādarāyaṇa, other than, like the previous section, suggesting that difference exists between those who want to seek the Brahman, and the Brahman who is the object of their aspirations.

TOPIC NINE: BREATH

1.3.39: *Kampanāt*

The breath (spoken of in Scriptural passages like *Kaṭha Upaniṣad* 6:2, refers to the Brahman) because of the trembling (or 'moving within' of the world suggested in that passage, which reads: 'this whole world, whatever there is, was created from and moves (or trembles) in Breath').

Having digressed on the subject of who is qualified to seek knowledge of the Brahman, Bādarāyaṇa now returns to the main topic of his work, the nature of the Brahman.

According to Rāmānuja and Nimbārka, this is a continuation of the section on the person the size of a thumb which preceded the digression on qualification for the Brahman knowledge. Since a digression of thirteen verses would seem to be rather out of character in a work as carefully structured as the *Brahma Sūtras*, we are inclined to accept Śaṅkara's position that *new* topical sections begin with 1.3.39.

The topical text referred to is *Kaṭha Upaniṣad* 6:2:

> This whole world, whatever there is,
> Was created from and moves (or trembles) in Breath (*prāṇa*).
> The great fear, the upraised thunderbolt,
> They who know that become immortal.

The question raised by this passage is whether *prāṇa* refers to the element breath or to the Brahman. Bādarāyaṇa responds that the reference is to the Brahman because of the reference to the whole world trembling in it, a reference that could apply to only the Brahman.

TOPIC TEN: LIGHT

1.3.40: *Jyotir darśanāt*

The light spoken of in Scriptural passages is the Brahman, because the Brahman (and not the element light) is the evident topic of those passages. (One such passage reads: 'As He shines, all else reflects His shining; all is resplendant with His splendor.' *Śvetāśvatara Upaniṣad* 6:14).

Although the expositors disagree as to the topical text for this verse, the *sūtra* clearly indicates that the word 'light' refers to the Brahman. Śaṅkara identifies the topical text as a passage in the *Chāndogya Upaniṣad* 8:12:3, where the highest light is described as that which is reached by souls. Rāmānuja, who considers this *sūtra* as part of the section dealing with the person the size of a thumb, believes that it refers to the *Kaṭha Upaniṣad*, while Nimbārka refers to the *Śvetāśvatara Upaniṣad*. In either case, the meaning is the same: light refers to the Brahman.

TOPIC ELEVEN: SPACE

1.3.41: *Ākāśo'rthāntaratvādivyapadeśāt*

The space of which Scripture speaks (in the passage which reads: 'Verily what is called space is the accomplisher of name and form. That within which they are included is the Brahman. That is the immortal. That is the self' *Chāndogya Upaniṣad* 8:14:1) is the Brahman, and not the soul, because that space is described as including name and form, as the Brahman itself, and as the immortal.

1.3.42: *Suṣuptyutkrāntyor bhedena*

But the soul is different, because of its state of deep sleep and egress from the body. (Scripture reveals characteristics distinct from the

Brahman's. The Brahman is all-knowing; the soul is sometimes unknowing, as in the state of deep sleep, with reference to which Scripture says 'the person within the embrace of the intelligent self knows nothing from within and without' *Bṛhadāraṇyaka Upaniṣad* 4:3:21. The Brahman is unchangeable, immortal, while the soul leaves the body. In Scriptures' words, 'Just as a heavily loaded cart moves creaking, even so the self in the body mounted by the self of the intelligence moves creaking, when one breathes with difficulty (at the moment of death).' *Bṛhadāraṇyaka Upaniṣad* 4:3:35).

1.3.43: *Patyādi śabdebhyaḥ*

(This difference is further accentuated by Scripture's use of) words like 'lord' when speaking of this Brahman-space, (as in the lines, 'In the space within the heart lies the controller of all, the lord of all, the ruler of all.' *Bṛhdāraṇyaka Upaniṣad* 4:4:22).

All expositors agree that the topical text comes from the *Chāndogya Upaniṣad* 8:14:1, as quoted above in *sūtra* 1.3.41. The question raised by this passage is whether space refers to the element or to the Brahman. Bādarāyaṇa replies that in this passage space is designated as something different from name and form, a designation that only could apply to the Brahman.

This is followed by 1.3.42, an important *sūtra* in that it strongly asserts that Difference exists between the Brahman and the individual soul as it exists in deep sleep. For the second time in the *Brahma Sūtras*, Bādarāyaṇa actually uses a form of the word for Difference, *bheda*. Even Śaṅkara interprets this *sūtra* as asserting Difference, although he and Rāmānuja differ in that he classifies the verse as part of the topic on Space. Both refer to *Bṛhadāraṇyaka Upaniṣad* 4:3:7, where there is discussion of the nature of the Self. *Sūtra* 1.3.43 confirms that the reference is to the Supreme Self, or the Brahman by calling attention to the words such as 'Lord' which describe this Self.

In these last three topics we see Bādarāyaṇa returning to an emphasis on the Brahman's difference from the world he has created. Topics nine, ten, and eleven, declare respectively that the Brahman is different from breath, light, and space. In addition, *sūtra* 1.3.42 provides us with one of Bādarāyaṇa's most definitive statements on the difference between the Brahman and the individual soul.

Finally, it should be noted that in 1.3.43 we see Bādarāyaṇa for the first time describe the Brahman in theistic terms through use of the word *pati*, or Lord. While Śaṅkara can object that such an understanding of the Brahman only exists at the lower level of truth, as we have indicated above in our discussion of the use of the doctrine of two truths as it applies to the Brahman and individual soul, there is no reason to believe that Bādarāyaṇa is writing from the perspective of two levels of truth unless he says so, and, considering that he makes no such statement, we are inclined to accept his words at face value.

FOOTNOES

1. See Appendix C for a listing of Bādarāyaṇa's techniques.
2. Monier-Williams, *Sanskrit-English Dictionary*, p. 763.
3. Ghate, *The Vedānta*, pp. 60–61.
4. See above, pp. 104–106.

CHAPTER VII

An Analysis of the *Brahma Sūtras* 1:4

TOPIC ONE: THE UNMANIFEST

1.4.1: *Ānumānikam apy ekeṣām iti cen na śarīrarūpakavinyastagṛhīter darśayati ca*

'Can it be that, as some maintain, the Unmanifest of which Scripture speaks (in the passage "Higher than the Great is the Unmanifest. Higher than the Unmanifest is the Person." *Kaṭha Upaniṣad* 3:11) is Prime Matter of the Sāṅkhyas' category known by inference (higher than which is the other Sāṅkhya category, the Person)?'

No, because it refers to what is contained in the metaphor of the body in the chariot (described earlier in the same Scripture in the lines 'Know the Self as the lord of the chariot and the body as, verily, the chariot.' *Kaṭha Upaniṣad* 3:3); in other words, to the Brahman.

1.4.2.: *Sūkṣmaṁ tu tad arhatvāt*

However, the subtle body is also the Unmanifest, as the meaning is appropriate.

1.4.3: *Tad adhīnatvād arthavāt*

The Unmanifest is intelligible as something dependent on the Brahman.

1.4.4: *Jñeyatvāvacanāc ca*

And the Unmanifest cannot refer to Prime Matter since there is no statement that the Unmanifest is an object of knowledge (as Prime Matter is in the Sāṅkhya system).

1.4.5: *Vadatīti cen na prājño hihi prakaraṇāt*

'Can it be argued that Scripture does speak of Prime Matter as an object of knowledge (in the words, "without sound, without touch, and without form, undecaying... without taste, eternal, without smell, without beginning, without end, beyond the great (*mahat*), abiding; by discerning that one is freed from the face of death.' *Kaṭha Upaniṣad* 3:15)?'

No, for the context reveals that the Self is being discussed.

1.4.6: *Trayāṇām eva caivam upanyāsaḥ praśnaś ca*

The context here is discussion and inquiry into three topics only (worship, the worshipper, and the worshipped), none of which includes Prime Matter.

1.4.7: *Mahadvac ca*

(Thus the word 'Unmanifest' has a clear Vedic meaning, though it has a Sāṅkhya sense too.) The same, is true of the word 'great' (*mahat*). (In the Sāṅkhya sense, it refers to the first evolute of Matter, Instinct, the Prodigious, or the Great. But, it has also a clear Vedic sense, as is seen in the wording of the *Kaṭha Upaniṣad*: 'Beyond the senses are the sense objects, and beyond the object is the mind, beyond the mind is the understanding, and beyond the understanding is the *great* Self.' *Kaṭha Upaniṣad* 3:10).

We find considerable disagreement between Madhva and the other expositors regarding the meaning of the fourth and final section (*pāda*), of the first chapter of the *Brahma Sūtras*, especially with regard to the first topic. Whereas Rāmānuja, Śaṅkara, and Nimbārka interpret this topic as a refutation of the Sāṅkhya theology, Madhva sees it as an analysis of words whose primary sense denotes something other than the Brahman. While this topic could include the Sāṅkhya categories which are examined by Rāmānuja, Śaṅkara, and Nimbārka, Madhva denies that this is the case. It is tempting to accept Madhva's position, particularly since he offers a rather convincing argument based on the structure of the *Brahma Sūtras*. Nonetheless, there are also two compelling reasons for rejecting Madhva's position. First, as we shall see below, a rather exaggerated and unorthodox interpretation of words in the topical text must be used in order to fit the text into Madhva's scheme. But secondly, and more importantly, if we accept Madhva's interpretation that *sūtras* 1.1.5 to 1.1.11 do not, as claimed by other expositors, deal with the Sāṅkhya doctrine, then nowhere in this first chapter is the Sāṅkhya doctrine addressed, a rather unlikely occurrence considering the significance of the Sāṅkhya challenge to Vedantic theology. Hence, we are inclined to accept Madhva's interpretation of 1.1.5 to 1.1.11, which does not deal with Sāṅkhya, and accept the other expositors' interpretation of 1.4.1 to 1.4.7, which does deal with Sāṅkhya. Furthermore, by rejecting the interpretation that *sūtras* 1.1.5 to 1.1.11 refer to Sāṅkhya, we avoid the problem of having two topical sections present lengthy discussions of the same issue.

All of the expositors, including Madhva, agree that the topical text for this section comes from the *Kaṭha Upaniṣad* 3:11:

> Higher than the Great is the Unmanifest (*avyakta*).
> Higher than the Unmanifest is the Person.
> Higher than the Person there is nothing at all.
> That is the goal. That is the highest course.

The references to the Unmanifest (*avyakta*) and the Person (*puruṣa*) strongly suggest Sāṅkhya doctrine, since these are basic categories of that doctrine in which the Unmanifest is Prime Matter and the Person is the spiritual power which activates Prime Matter to cause creation.

Madhva responds that the Unmanifest refers to the Brahman, a rather unlikely interpreation since the text declares that the Person is *higher* than the Unmanifest. Madhva's strained explanation is that, like all terms, 'Unmanifest' can refer both to itself *and* to the Brahman who dwells within it. But Madhva fails to explain why the text would use the word in a manner in which one of its two meanings (i.e., the Brahman) is entirely inappropriate within the text.

Given the problems presented by Madhva's intepretation, we are inclined to accept that of Rāmānuja and Śaṅkara. Thus, 1.4.1 declares that the Unmanifest refers to the body, not Prime Matter, since this can be deduced by comparing the elements listed in the text with an earlier *Kaṭha* verse that uses a chariot metaphor. By a process of elimination, it can be seen that the Unmanifest refers to the body of the person who drives the chariot. In response to the objection that the term Unmanifest cannot apply to the body, which is manifest, the reply in 1.4.2 is that the reference is to be charioteer's *subtle* body, from which the manifest body is produced. In response to this, another objection is raised, namely that if the body referred to is an

Unmanifest one, then cannot that be the same as the Sāṅkhyan category? Bādarāyaṇa responds in 1.4.3 that this cannot be the case, since the Unmanifest cannot refer to Prime Matter since, according to Sāṅkhya doctrine, Prime Matter is an object of liberating knowledge, but there is no injunction in the text to know the Unmanifest. *Sūtra* 1.4.5 adds that since the Unmanifest is associated with the intelligent Self, it cannot be Prime Matter which lacks intelligence. Bādarāyaṇa further supports his interpretation in 1.4.6 by pointing out that three topics are mentioned in the text from the *Kaṭha Upaniṣad*, none of which is the Prime Matter. Finally, Bādarāyaṇa closes the section with 1.4.7, in which he remarks that just as the word 'great' (*mahat*) can have one meaning in the Sāṅkhya system and a different meaning in Vedantic theology, the same also is true for the word 'Unmanifest'.

The significance of this section for our investigation of Bādarāyaṇa's theology lies in the clear rejection of the Sāṅkhya philosophy. Even if, as we believe, verses 1.1.5 to 1.1.11 do not refute Sāṅkhya, this section of the *Brahma Sūtras* does. By rejecting Sāṅkhya, Bādarāyaṇa thereby affirms the converse of Sāṅkhyan doctrine, namely that one being is both the primary and efficient cause of creation, that creation proceeds from a personal God, and that spirit and matter are united in God rather than existing as eternally separate entities. We see this personal nature of the Brahman referred to in 1.4.5, which speaks of his intelligence. It is significant to remember that the last verse of the third section of the first chapter also inferred the personal nature of the Brahman by use of the word Lord (*pati*). It also should be noted that even though Bādarāyaṇa rejects the pure dualism of the Sāṅkhya school, the unity he affirms continues to be one in which the separate nature of the members of the unity is preserved. In this section, for example, by asserting in 1.4.3 that the unmanifest subtle body is *dependent* on the Brahman, Bādarāyaṇa affirms the difference that is a necessary corollary of any relationship in which one entity is dependent upon another.

TOPIC TWO: THE UNBORN

1.4.8: *Camasavad aviśeṣāt*

The She Goat/Unborn Female of the Scriptural passage ('The She Goat/Unborn Female, red, white, and black, produces manifold offspring in her likeness—the He Goat/Unborn Male lies with her and enjoys himself,' *Śvetāśvatara Upaniṣad* 4:5) does not signify the Prime Matter of the Sāṅkhyas, because she lacks the specific qualities of the Sāṅkhya PrimeMatter. In an analogous way, Scripture talks about the 'bowl' ('with its mouth below and bottom up. In it is placed the glory of manifold forms.' *Bṛhadāraṇyaka Upaniṣad* 2:2:3. We do not know what this metaphor specifically refers to until Scripture itself tells us, "What is called 'the bowl with its mouth below and bottom up' is the head... breaths, verily, are where the glory of manifold forms is placed..." With regard to the metaphor of the She Goat, however, Scripture does not specify in the context).

1.4.9: *Jyotirupakramā tu tathā hy adhīyata eke*

And the unborn one has her origin in light (the Brahman), as some read in other passages (as in the *Bṛhadāraṇyaka Upaniṣad* 4:4:16: 'That before which the year revolves with its days, that the gods revere as the light of lights, as life immortal).'

1.4.10: *Kalpanopadeśāc ca madhvādivad avirodhaḥ*

The metaphor (whereby white, red, and black, or the three Attributes of Brightness, Passion, and Darkness are identified with the She Goat) is not contradictory, like the example of honey (metaphorically identified by Scripture with the sun, also without contradiction).

This short section consisting of only three verses appears to be based on a topical text from the *Śvetāśvatara Upaniṣad* 4:5, quoted above in *sūtra* 1.4.8.

We find here a rather puzzling verse that presents a challenge to Bādarāyaṇa's thesis that all words referring to the highest being who is creator of the world refer to the Brahman. The text refers to an unborn She-Goat (*ajā*) as the source of creation, along with a male principle that interacts with her. The reference to *two* principles associated with creation suggests Sāṅkhya doctrine, as does the reference to the three colours which correspond to the Sāṅkhya attributes of Passion, Brightness, and Darkness. These strong similarities to Sāṅkhya doctrine lead us to accept the interpretation shared by Rāmānuja and Śaṅkara that this section continues Bādarāyaṇa's refutation of texts which appear to refer to Sāṅkhya, as opposed to Madhva's interpretation that this section deals with passages that refer to various sacrifices.

In 1.4.8, Bādarāyaṇa appears to argue that, since there is no specific indication in the text that the She-Goat refers to Prime Matter as creator, and since other sections of the text indicate that the Brahman is the topic, then we can conclude that the She-Goat is a metaphorical reference to the Brahman. *Camasavat* means that this is analogous to another passage in the Upaniṣads (apparently *Bṛhadāraṇyaka Upaniṣad* 2:2:3) where the meaning of the word 'bowl' can only be understood by referring to surrounding passages.

Śāṅkara and Rāmānuja present two equally tenable interpretations of *sūtra* 1.4.10. According to Rāmānuja, it means that the text indicates that the unborn one originates in light, or the Brahman, which means that she is dependent, and therefore cannot be identified as Prime Matter which is independent. Śaṅkara believes that the unborn female refers to the elements, beginning with light. Śaṅkara appears to offer the more convincing interpretation of *sūtra* 1.4.10, in that he sees it as addressing the obvious question of how can the supreme Brahman be referred to as a She-Goat. The answer is that Scripture shows that the Brahman can be referred to in a metaphorical sense, as in the case of the sun being referred to as 'honey' for the gods.

TOPIC THREE: THE FIVE GROUPS OF FIVE

1.4.11: *Na Sāṅkhyopasamgrahād api nānābhāvād atirekāc ca*

('You Vedantins cannot reject the 25 categories of Sāṅkya, which are established in and include the basic Sāṅkya category, Prime Matter, for these categories are endorsed by your own Scripture with the words, "that in which the five groups of five and space are established that alone I regard as the Self".' *Bṛhadāraṇyaka Upaniṣad* 4:4:17).

The reference to twenty-five does not prove that Scripture endorses Sāṅkhya, because the Sāṅkhya categories are different and the categories mentioned in Scripture exceed twenty-five. (The Sāṅkhya categories are discrete, while those of Scripture are combined in groups of five; the Sāṅkhya total is 25, while that of Scripture is 27, that is, the five groups of five plus space and the Self).

1.4.12: *Prāṇādayo vākyaśeṣāt*

The groups of five, including the life-breath and the others, are described in the passage following (the one quoted above, which, in the *Mādhyaṁdina* rescension reads: 'The life of life, the eye of the eye, the ear of the ear, the food of the food and the mind of the mind' *Bṛhadāraṇyaka Upaniṣad* 4:4:18).

1.4.13: *Jyotiṣaikeṣām asaty anne*

In the rescension of some (the *Kāṇvas*) the phrase 'food of food' is missing, but the 'light of light' that is in its place completes the number five.

Bādarāyaṇa continues his rejection of Sāṇkhya doctrine, this time with reference to a passage found in the *Bṛhadāraṇyaka Upaniṣad* 4:4:17:

That in which the five groups of five
And space are established,
That alone I, the knowing, I, the immortal,
Believe to be the Self, the immortal Brahman.

The position is raised that the passage refers to five groups of five, or a total of twenty-five, suggesting that the passage refers to the Sāṅkhya categories, which also number twenty-five.

In 1.4.11, Bādarāyaṇa rejects this position for two reasons. First, the Scriptural passage refers to five groups of five; the Sāṅkhya categories are each separate and are not combined into five groups. Secondly, since the Self and space are referred to in the passage, in addition to the five groups of five, the total number of entities referred to is twenty-seven, not twenty-five.

In 1.4.12, Bādarāyaṇa explains that the five groups refer to the breath eye, ear, food, and mind, as seen in the *Bṛhadāraṇyaka Upaniṣad* 4:4:18. In response to the objection that in some rescensions there is no reference to food and hence the number of categories would not equal five, Bādarāyaṇa replies in 1.4.13 that in such rescensions, there is reference to light as the fifth category.

TOPIC FOUR: THE BRAHMAN AS CREATOR

1.4.14: *Kāraṇatvena cākāśādiṣu yathāvyapadiṣṭokeḥ*

The Brahman (and not Prime Matter) is the creator because Scripture declares that He, as described, is the cause of space, etc.

1.4.15: *Samākarṣāt*

We know that descriptions of creation from non-being refer to the Brahman because of the connection with passages referring to the Brahman as creator.

Bādarāyaṇa now takes up the Sāṅkhya challenge to the Vedāntic doctrine of creation. The argument on the Sāṅkhya side is that its school has a clear creative principle, Prime Matter, and a clear sequence of evolutes. The Vedānta, on the other hand, has no clear idea of what is the ultimate cause, or the order of creation. Some Vedāntic texts claim that it is Being, others that it is non-Being, the Self, space, breath, etc. According to the Sāṅkhyas, this Vedāntic confusion proves the truth of the Sāṅkhya's position. To this Bādarāyaṇa replies that in some *sūtras* the Brahman is defined in his essential qualities, and in others in his causal qualities (*kāraṇatvena*), but it is always the Brahman who is indicated as the ultimate cause.

Sūtra 1.4.14 is somewhat unusual, in that it does not refer to any single topical text. Rather, according to Śaṅkara and Rāmānuja, the *sūtra* refers to the several passages which, at first glance, appear to call into question the doctrine of the Brahman as creator of the world. According to Śaṅkara, in 1.4.14 Bādarāyaṇa addresses the challenge posed by the different *orders* of creation found in various scriptural passages. Rāmānuja, in contrast, believes that this *sūtra* examines those passages that refer to creation from non-being (*asat*). In either case, the *sūtra* clearly reaffirms that the Brahman is indeed the cause of creation, although no specific reasons are given to support this position.

In 1.4.15, we find an example of the 'one word *sūtra*': *samākarṣāt*. Needless to say, arriving at an interpretation of such *sūtras* is an impossible task without referring to the ideas of the expositors. If we follow the positions of Śaṅkara and Rāmānuja, the reference here is to the *Taittirīya Upaniṣad* 2:7, which describes creation as originating from non-being. Bādarāyaṇa affirms that this is actually a reference to the Brahman, as is seen from the connection of non-being with other passages that clearly refer to the Brahman.

TOPIC FIVE: WHOSE WORK IS THE WORLD

1.4.16: *Jagadvācitvāt*

In speaking about the world's maker, Scripture denotes the

Brahman. (The world is referred to as the persons in the sun, moon, lightning, thunder, air, space, fire, water, mirror, shadow, echo, sound, the body, the right eye and the left eye. These, Scripture declares through Ajātaśatru, are not the Brahman, but only 'He, verily, O Bālāki, who is the maker of these persons (whom you have mentioned in succession), he of whom all this is the work, he alone is to be known.') *Kauṣītaki Upaniṣad* 4:19.

1.4.17: *Jīvamukhyaprāṇaliṅgām neti*
cet tad vyākhyātam

'May it be that Scripture is not speaking of the Brahman because it alludes to the characteristics of the self and the chief breath? (It refers to the characteristics of the self thus: 'Just as a chief enjoys his own men, or as his own men are of service to a chief, even so this sense of intelligence enjoys these selves, even so these selves are of service to that self.' *Kauṣitaki Upaniṣad* 4:20, And to the characteristics of the chief breath thus: 'Then in this life breath alone he becomes one.' *Ibid.*)?

This relationship of the self and the chief breath to the Brahman has already been explained (in 1.1.31).

1.4.18: *Anyārtham tu Jaiminiḥ praśnavyākhyānābhyām*
api caivam eke

But Jaimini thinks that the reference to the individual soul has another meaning because of Ajātaśatru's question to Bālāki and Ajātaśatru's own answer. (In the *Kauṣītaki Upaniṣad* 4:19 the question which Ajātaśatru put to Bālāki, when he woke up a sleeping man was: 'Where in this case, O Bālāki, has this person lain... from where has he returned?' As Bālāki was unable to reply, Ajātaśatru declared 'While asleep he has no dreams whatever,' thus proclaiming the Vedantic doctrine that the soul becomes one with the Brahman in dreamless sleep.) Other texts have similar readings (The Vājasaneyins, for example, to the question, 'Where has this person lain... from where has he returned?' respond 'He lies in the space within the heart.')

The topic of creation again comes into play in the fifth topic of this section. According to Śaṅkara and Rāmānuja, Bādarāyaṇa bases this section on a text from the *Kauṣītaki Upaniṣad* 4:19: 'He, verily, Oh Bālāki, who is the maker of these persons whom you have mentioned in succession, of whom, verily, this is the work—He, verily, should be known.'

The question arises as to whether this passage might refer to the elements, which are mentioned in earlier passages, or the individual soul, which is known as the maker of works (*karma*). Bādarāyaṇa responds in *sūtra* sixteen that the reference is to the Brahman since the passage indicates that the world is His work, and this feat could only be performed by the Brahman.

In *sūtra* 1.4.17, Bādarāyaṇa responds to the objection that there are clear references in the text to the breath and the individual soul. Employing a technique that we have seen used in 1.3.21, Bādarāyaṇa states that the objection has already been explained by the content of another *sūtra*, presumably 1.1.31.

The opinions of Bādarāyaṇa's contemporary, Jaimini, again appear in 1.4.18. Jaimini appears to offer another explanation of the apparent reference to the individual soul, that being that in the question and answer section that follows the topical text, the discussion leads to the conclusion that the Brahman resides in, and in some senses is identical to, the individual soul. Hence, a reference to the individual soul can actually be a reference to the Brahman, in that the Brahman resides in and controls the soul.

It is interesting to note that Madhva offers a much different interpretation of these *sūtras*. Combining them with *sūtras* nineteen through twenty-one, he interprets this section as defending the doctrine that words can have a dual meaning, referring both to the Brahman and to the created reality which they more commonly denote. That Madhva could produce a fairly convincing interpretation of these *sūtras* that differs sharply from that of other expositors, such as Śaṅkara and Rāmānuja, is a compelling illustration of the ambiguity of the *sūtras* and their capacity for providing many different interpretations. In this case, we find Śaṅkara's and Rāmānuja's interpretation slightly more convincing, although, as demonstrated by Sharma, Madhva's interpretation also is well taken.[1]

Assuming the validity of the interpretation of Śaṅkara and Rāmānuja, this section, along with the previous one, provides us with further evidence that in Bādarāyaṇa's own theology, the Brahman's role as creator was perceived as one of His primary qualities, if not His single most important quality. From the first description of the Brahman in 1.1.2, on through numerous other sections, we find Bādarāyaṇa repeatedly refer to the Brahman as creator, and, furthermore, asserting that it is this quality of world-creating that distinguishes Him from all other beings. As we have argued in earlier sections, defining the Brahman as creator inherently affirms that He is somehow different from the created world. On the other hand, Jaimini's remarks in 1.4.18 remind us that Bādarāyaṇa also perceives the existence of *some* type of Identity between the Brahman and His creation, though neither here nor elsewhere in the *Brahma Sūtras* is this Identity described with any significant clarity.

TOPIC SIX: THE SELF TO BE SEEN, HEARD, ETC.

1.4.19: *Vākyānvayāt*

The Self proclaimed by Scripture (in the long passage which ends with the words: 'Verily, the Self, Maitreyī, is to be seen, to be heard, to be reflected upon, to be meditated upon,' *Bṛhadāraṇyaka Upaniṣad* 4:5:6) is the Higher Self, because that is the tenor of the sentences (of the entire passage; there husband, wife, sons, wealth, cattle, the Brahmins, the Kṣatriyas, the world, the gods, the Vedas, the beings and indeed all are declared to be dear not for their own sake, but for the sake of the Self; and the Self in this passage clearly transcends the 'all').

1.4.20: *Pratijñāsiddher liṅgam Āśmarathyaḥ*

For Āśmarathya, the proposition that the knowledge of one thing leads to the knowledge of all (proclaimed by Scripture in the lines: 'by one clod of clay, all that is made of clay becomes known' *Chāndogya Upaniṣad* 6:1:4) is proof that the knowledge of the individual soul refers to that of the higher Self.

1.4.21: *Utkramiṣyatah evam bhāvād ity Auḍulomiḥ*

According to Auḍulomi, the individual soul is identified with the Brahman because the soul becomes such when it departs from the body. (As Scripture declares: 'Just as the flowing rivers disappear in the ocean carrying off name and shape, even so the knower, freed from name and shape, attains to the divine person, higher than the high.' *Muṇḍaka Upaniṣad* 3:2:8).

1.4.22: *Avastither iti Kāśakṛtsnaḥ*

According to Kāśakṛtsnaḥ, the individual soul is identified with the

Brahman because the Brahman abides within the soul. (In Scripture's words: 'He who dwells in the understanding/soul, yet is other than understanding/soul, whom the understanding/soul does not know... he is your self, the inner controller, the immortal' *Bṛhadāraṇyaka Upaniṣad* 3:7:27).

In this section Bādarāyaṇa draws his topical text from the *Bṛhadāraṇyaka Upaniṣad* 4:5:6, in which the great teacher Yājñavalkya teaches his wife, Maitreyī, about the nature of the Self. After a series of twelve statements in which Yājñavalkya states that finite objects are not loved for their own sake, but rather for the sake of the Self, he adds:

> 'Lo, verily, it is the Self that should be seen, that should be hearkened to,that should be thought on, that should be pondered on, Oh Maitreyī.'

The question arises as to what this Self refers. It is the individual soul, the Sāṅkhya *puruṣa*, or the Highest Self, the Brahman?

In 1.4.19, Bādarāyaṇa presumably affirms that the reference is to the Highest Self, since when one connects surrounding passages with 4:5:6, it becomes apparent that only the Highest Self could be referred to. In essence, Bādarāyaṇa establishes his point by argument from context, a method which he employs frequently through the *Brahma Sūtras*.

This *sūtra* also illustrates the ambiguity that is characteristic of the *Brahma Sūtras*. The *sūtra* contains only two words combined into one compound in the ablative case: *vākya-anvayāt*. The general, literal meaning of the compound is apparent: 'because of the connection of the sentences.' However, there is no indication of the *topic* to which the words refer. In other words, there is no clue regarding what is proven or demonstrated by the 'connection of the sentences'. Of course, the traditional—and reasonable—practice in interpreting *sūtras* where the subject is absent, is to assume that the subject is the Brahman. Nonetheless, the fact that the subject is not explicitly stated allows considerable leeway in interpreting the *sūtra*, and provides the various sectarian theologians with an opportunity to read their own theologies into Bādarāyaṇa's work.

The remaining three *sūtras* of this section address the problem of the close association of the individual soul and the Highest Self, as found in the topical text. Each *sūtra* offers the opinion of a different sage. In 1.4.20, Āśmarathya offers the opinion that since Scripture declares that through one thing all things are known, therefore it is appropriate to refer to the Brahman through finite realities such as the individual soul, inasmuch as He is present in them and represents their essence. In 1.4.21, Auḍulomi argues that it is appropriate to identify the individual soul with the Brahman, since after leaving the body at death (*utkramiṣyata*), the soul becomes united with the Brahman:

Finally, in 1.4.22 we hear the opinion of Kāśakṛtsna, who states that the identification of the individual soul with the Brahman is possible because of the soul's 'abiding in' (*avasthites*) the Brahman. This is a very significant *sūtra*, in that it clearly asserts some type of Identity between the Brahman and the individual soul. How one interprets that Identity depends on how one interprets the word *avasthithes.* Śaṅkara interprets the *sūtra* as affirming that the Brahman also exists in the condition of the individual soul, a condition which, of course, is ultimately unreal. Hence, he sees the *sūtra* as a statement of pure Identity. In contrast, Rāmānuja believes that the *sūtra* refers to the Brahman as abiding or dwelling within the soul, which is real and distinct from the Brahman. Typically, Bādarāyaṇa provides us with no help in clarifying his meaning. However, we are inclined to concur with Rāmānuja, based on the connotations of *avasthita.* Monier-Williams identifies some of its meanings as 'standing near, placed, having its place or abode.'[2] The root of the word is the verb *sthā*, which can mean to stand, to stay, to abide by, to be near, etc. With this verb, there is a sense of *location*, implying one object in close proximity to another object. While there clearly is a connotation of closeness, there is no connotation of Identity. Indeed, the very nature of the concept of location implies some type of duality between two objects that stand in relationship to each other. Thus, given the meaning of *avasthita*, it would appear far more likely that Kāśakṛtsna is referring to the Brahman abiding in the individual soul, rather than the Brahman being identical with the individual soul.

This is a rather important section of the *Brahma Sūtras* since in it Bādarāyaṇa clearly affirms a belief in some type of Identity. Nonetheless, as in other parts of his work, he fails to clarify the precise nature of that Identity and its relationship to Difference. Ghate's remark about Bādarāyaṇa's use of *avasthita* could apply to many other sections of the *Brahma Sūtras:* 'Very probably the advocate of this view, *not having any definite solution of the problem*, used a general word to explain the relation between the Brahman and *jīva*."[3]

TOPIC SEVEN: THE MATERIAL AND EFFICIENT CAUSE

1.4.23: *Prakṛtiś ca pratijñadṛṣṭāntānuparodhāt*

The Brahman is the material and efficient cause of the world, because there is no conflict between the proposition ('by it the inaudible becomes audible, the imperceptible, the perceived, the unknowable, the known' as Scripture states in *Chāndogya Upaniṣad* 6:13) and the example ('Through a single lump of clay all that is fashioned from clay is known. The changes are only verbal, a mere matter of name: only clay is the reality.' *Chāndogya Upaniṣad* 6:1:4).

1.4.24: *Abhidhyopadeśāc ca*

And this is seen from the statements about his reflecting to become many (statements like the following: 'It thought, May I be many, may I grow forth'. *Chāndogya Upaniṣad* 6:2:3).

1.4.25: *Śakṣāc cobhayāmnānāt*

That the Brahman is both material and efficient cause is directly stated in the sacred text (as, for instance, in the following passage: 'What was the word, what the tree from which they shaped heaven and earth? You wise ones, search in your minds, whereon it stood, supporting the worlds. Brahman was the wood, Brahman the tree from which they shaped heaven and earth; you wise ones, it stood on Brahman, supporting the worlds.').

1.4.26: *Ātmakṛteḥ pariṇāmāt*

The Brahman is both efficient and material cause, because, (as efficient cause) he acts upon himself (and thus becomes his own material cause. As Scripture says: 'Thereupon, verily, was existence produced. That made itself into a soul' *Taittirīya Upaniṣad* 2:7). This Self-causation is a transformation (of his pre-existent reality).

1.4.27: *Yoniś ca hi gīyate*

And the Brahman is material cause because he is proclaimed to be the source/womb (in Scriptural passages like: 'That which is ungraspable, without family, without caste, without sight or hearing, without hands and feet, eternal, all-pervading, exceedingly subtle, that is the Undecaying which the wise perceive as the source/womb of beings.' *Muṇḍaka Upaniṣad* 1:1:6).

Having made numerous references to the Brahman as creator, Bādarāyaṇa now closes the first of the *Brahma Sūtras*' four chapters with a clarification of the precise nature of the Brahman's creatorship. Hence, this section serves as a very useful tool in our attempt to arrive at a more specific understanding of Bādarāyaṇa's view of the relationship between the Brahman and the world.

Unlike most sections, this one is not based on a single topical text but rather on several texts that express the same idea. Śaṅkara, for instance, identifies *Praśna Upaniṣad* 6:3:4, while Rāmānuja refers to several different passages. The common theme of all the passages is reference to the Brahman's act of creating the world, and the specific question that Bādarāyaṇa addresses is whether Scripture describes the Brahman as the material cause, the efficient cause, or both. More specifically, while Scripture clearly portrays the Brahman as efficient cause, there is some doubt as to how the pure Brahman could be the material cause of our impure world.

In 1.4.23, Bādarāyaṇa declares that the Brahman is the material, as well as the efficient cause, since only if the Brahman is the material cause can there by agreement with the Scriptural premise that through one thing all things are known (*Chāndogya Upaniṣad* 6:1:4). If the Brahman were not the material cause, then knowing Him would not lead to knowing all things about the world, just as knowledge of the potter does not necessarily lead to knowledge of his pots. In order for the Scriptural statement to be true, the Brahman must be the material as well as the efficient cause.

In the next *sūtra*, 1.4.24, Bādarāyaṇa refers to passages which describe the Brahman as reflecting on the desire to become many. These passages confirm that the Brahman is the efficient cause, in that creation is caused by his decision to create, and also the material cause, since creation involves a transformation of his own being.

Sūtra 1.4.25 affirms the same point, although differing interpretations are possible. Śaṅkara believes that Bādarāyaṇa states that the Brahman is efficient and material cause since Scripture describes Him as *both* (*ubhaya*) the origin and dissolution of the world. Rāmānuja, however, interprets ***ubhaya*** as referring to the Brahman as *both* efficient and material cause, with the *sūtra* stating that Scripture clearly and directly describes the Brahman as such. We are inclined to accept Rāmānuja's interpretation, since the 'both' with which he associates *ubhaya*, namely material and efficient causality, is found as a pairing in the two previous *sūtras*, whereas as Śaṅkara's pairing (creation and dissolution) is newly introduced.

Sūtra 1.4.26 refers to a passage in *Taittirīya Upaniṣad* 2:7, where the Brahman is described as creating from itself, a clear indication that the Brahman is the material cause of the world. Bādarāyaṇa adds that this is accomplished through *pariṇāma*, which means transformation or modification. Unfortunately, Bādarāyaṇa does not provide us with any of the details of the nature of this modification. Hence, Rāmānuja interprets it as a reference to his soul-body analogy, while Śaṅkara declines to comment on the nature of this modification.

Finally, Bādarāyaṇa closes the section by arguing that the Brahman must be the material cause of the world since He is referred to as its womb or source (*yoni*), a word which has obvious connotations of material causality.

Looking at this section with reference to our task of identifying Bādarāyaṇa's own theology, we see signs of both Difference and Identity. On the one hand, by asserting the Brahman's role as creator Bādarāyaṇa affirms some element of Difference between creator and creation. However, this section makes clear that Bādarāyaṇa perceives creation in a manner that preserves an element of Identity. This is not the type of creation in which the creator acts as efficient cause on a separate and distinct entity that serves as the material cause. By asserting that the Brahman is the material as well as the efficient cause, Bādarāyaṇa makes a strong statement on Identity. There is not, however, any evidence to suggest that Bādarāyaṇa perceives this Identity to be similar to that found in Śaṅkara's theology, where Identity is established by denying the reality of the created world. Quite to the contrary, there is a strong element of *realism* in Bādarāyaṇa's thought: *both* the Brahman and the world are real, in some ways different from each other and in some ways identical to each other. Apparently the Brahman's capacity to create a real world which is distinct from yet still part of Himself, is accomplished through some type of modification (*pariṇāma*), as alluded in 1.4.26, the precise nature of which Bādarāyaṇa does not describe.

TOPIC EIGHT: CLOSING

1.4.28: *Etena sarve vyākhyātā vyākhyātāḥ*

Thus, all of the objections are explained by this section.

Here Bādarāyaṇa simply closes the section, repeating the final word for a sense of finality.

FOOTNOTES

1. B.N.K. Sharma, *The Brahma Sūtras*, 1:295–302.
2. Monier-Williams, *A Sanskrit-English Dictionary*, p. 106.
3. Ghate, *The Vedānta*, p. 67.

CHAPTER VIII

Conclusion

PRELIMINARY CONSIDERATIONS

Having examined each of the *sūtras* which comprise the first of the *Brahma Sūtras*' four chapters, we can now attempt to summarize what these *sūtras* reveal about Bādarāyaṇa's own theology. A few cautionary notes are, however, in order.

First, we must remember that our conclusions are based solely on the first chapter of the *Brahma Sūtras*, and should not be interpreted as a definitive and final account of Bādarāyaṇa's complete theology. Our conclusions reflect only the first chapter of his work, and hence do not address Bādarāyaṇa's positions on the means of liberation (*mārga*) which are found in the third chapter, and the fruits of liberation (*phalam*) which are found in the fourth chapter. Nor do our conclusions take into account the statements about the nature of the Brahman found in chapter two. Nonetheless, while our *sūtra*-by-*sūtra* analysis is limited to the *Brahma Sūtras*' first chapter, we will examine in a brief and more general sense the theology of the remaining three chapters since, as we shall see later in this section, these final three chapters tend to express the same theological positions found in our analysis of the first chapter.

It also should be noted that our conclusions regarding Bādarāyaṇa's own theology are based solely on his own words as found in the *Brahma Sūtras*. This approach differs considerably from the sectarian expositors who relied on years of oral tradition to provide detail and comprehensiveness in Bādarāyaṇa's theology. When stripped of the tradition that has been attached to it, we find that the *Brahma Sūtras* express some rather clear but *general* theological positions, which is in sharp contrast to the complex theologies presented by the expositors. In other words, Bādarāyaṇa makes statements about the nature of the Brahman, but he does not analyze or expand upon, or for that matter, even defend his statements in any great detail. The complicated theologies that explain the Brahman's relationship to the world are the creations of the expositors, and are not to be found anywhere in the *Brahma Sūtras*. The theology that we find in the *Brahma Sūtras* is a rather simple theology, free of complicated and abstruse explanations, and that is the only type of theology that we will find if we confine our analysis to the words of Bādarāyaṇa. Thus, while we will draw conclusions regarding what Bādarāyaṇa believes about certain theological issues, there are many other issues about which we can only say that Bādarāyaṇa expresses no position at all. There is a leanness about Bādarāyaṇa's theology which stands in sharp contrast to the baroque theologizing of Śaṅkara, Rāmānuja, and the other expositors.

Consideration also must be given to the fact that the difficulty of arriving at definitive translations of Bādarāyaṇa's *sūtras* makes it equally difficult to discern a definitive theology expressed by the *Brahma Sūtras*. The various hindrances associated with translating the *sūtras*, described in the first chapter of this work, make it difficult to piece together the exact contents of Bādarāyaṇa's own theology. Appendix B, for example, summarizes the remarkable brevity and conciseness of the *sūtra* style of writing. In the first chapter of the *Brahma Sūtras*, we find an average of less than five words per *sūtra*. When minor words such as conjunctions and adverbs are not counted, we find an average of barely three words per *sūtra*. Eighteen *sūtras* contain only two or fewer words, while three *sūtras* contain only one word. If comprehensive theological statements are being made in the *Brahma Sūtras*, then surely many words are left out of the *written Brahma Sūtras* since such a comprehensive theology cannot be articulated through such short sentences.

BĀDARĀYAṆA'S METHODOLOGIES

Before looking at the content of Bādarāyaṇa's theology, let us first examine the various methodologies that are found in the *Brahma Sūtras*, since one of the more interesting aspects of this work is the use of many different methodologies by Bādarāyaṇa.

Basically, we find that Bādarāyaṇa employs six different methodologies:

1. Proof by reference to qualities; Clearly the technique used most frequently by Bādarāyaṇa, this method consists of proving that a topical text refers to the Brahman by identifying qualities or attributes listed in the text that clearly apply to the Brahman. Doubt about the meaning of a passage is removed

by demonstrating that qualities applicable only to the Brahman are present in the passage.

Bādarāyaṇa employs this technique in at least twenty-five *sūtras* in the first chapter of the *Brahma Sūtras*. In some *sūtras*, the attribute in question is stated in the *sūtra*. In 1.3.16, for instance, Bādarāyaṇa proves that the small space in the heart refers to the Brahman by demonstrating that the small space is described as having the attribute of supporting (*dhṛtes*) the world, a quality that can apply only to the Brahman. In many *sūtras*, however, the quality in question is alluded to but not actually stated in the *sūtra*, leaving the interpreter to determine which quality was meant by Bādarāyaṇa. In 1.3.9, for example, Bādarāyaṇa states that the 'abundance' (*bhūman*) refers to the Brahman on the grounds that the qualities associated with the *bhūman* apply only to the Brahman. The *sūtra*, however, does not list these qualities; literally it simply reads, 'And because of the applicability of the qualities' (*dharmopapttes ca*).

It is interesting to note that this method operates under the assumption that certain qualities unquestionably apply to the Brahman. Bādarāyaṇa appears to take for granted that these qualities apply only to the Brahman. Hence, by identifying these qualities, we can deduce part of the content of Bādarāyaṇa's own theology. To do so now would be a bit premature inasmuch as this is the subject of our next section, but we can briefly note that the qualities which Bādarāyaṇa assumes are inherent to the Brahman tend to be qualities which assert his uniqueness from, and hence his difference from, the rest of creation. Specifically, Bādarāyaṇa appears to assume that any reference to the creator and sustainer of the world, and the being who is the goal of those who seek liberation, must be necessarily refer to the Brahman.

2. Proof by context: On several occasions, Bādarāyaṇa proves his point by reference to the broader context in which the passage in question occurs. In 1.4.5, for example, he demonstrates that the questionable passage refers to the Brahman on the grounds that the topic of the section in which the passage occurs is the Brahman.

3. Proof by use of symbolism: Occasionally, Bādarāyaṇa attempts to demonstrate that a passage refers to the Brahman

by alluding to the use of symbolic language for the purpose of meditation and devotion. This is a useful technique in interpreting passages which, at face value, appear to refer to something other than the Brahman.

4. Proof by appeal to Scripture: On ten occasion Bādarāyaṇa makes his point by referring to other Scriptural passages which support his position. In at least five of these instances, Bādarāyaṇa refers to passages in Sacred Tradition (*Smṛti*) rather than Revelation (*Śrūti*).

5. Appeal to general knowledge: In two *sūtras* (1.23.1 and 1.3.17), Bādarāyaṇa employs the rather interesting (and, from a strictly logical perspective, unsound) method of proving his point by pointing out that common knowledge acknowledges it to be true. The obvious fault with Bādarāyaṇa's use of this technique is that one cannot conclude from the fact that most people hold a given view, that that view therefore is true, since it is quite possible for most, and even all people, to be mistaken. The popularity of a position is not proof of its validity.

6. Proof by reference to other authorities: Finally, Bādarāyaṇa occasionally calls upon other respected authorities to demonstrate his position. In ten *sūtras* in the first chapter, Bādarāyaṇa refers to other theologians, although in some of these references the theologian is credited with a view that is rejected by Bādarāyaṇa.

THE THEOLOGY OF THE BRAHMA SŪTRAS: CHAPTER ONE

We turn now to a summary of what can be deduced about the content of Bādarāyaṇa's own theology. As indicated above, the conclusions that we can reach are rather general in nature, since Bādarāyaṇa simply does not elaborate on his ideas in the manner of the expositors. Nonetheless, while we can make only general conclusions about the content of Bādarāyaṇa's own theology, we can do so with considerable confidence that they do indeed reflect Bādarāyaṇa's thought. What Bādarāyaṇa says is not detailed, but it is consistent. The *sūtras* of the first chapter consistently reflect the same basic theological positions, however general and lacking in detail those positions might be.

More specifically, the *Brahma Sūtras* express a theology that affirms the reality of both the Brahman and the world, a relationship between the Brahman and the world that is characterized by both Difference *and* Identity: Difference in the sense that the Brahman and the world of souls and matter are separate beings with different qualities; Identity in the sense that the Brahman is somehow present within this world which he has created and continues to control from within. The Brahman and the world are presented as realities which are intimately related to eah other in a dependent/independent, creator/created, controller/controlled relationship, and, indeed, perhaps in other ways as well, although Bādarāyaṇa does not go into any detail in defining this relationship. Thus, the explanations of the expositors, however clever they may be, must be seen as their own inventions and not the theology of Bādarāyaṇa.

Within the context of asserting that Bādarāyaṇa advocates a type of Difference-in-Identity, it must be added that the focus of the *Brahma Sūtras* clearly is on asserting the Brahman's Difference from the world. While acknowledging both Difference and Identity, in the majority of his *sūtras* Bādarāyaṇa endeavours to demonstrate that the Brahman is different from his creation. Thus, there are approximately sixty-five *sūtras* in the first chapter which assert Difference as the nature of the Brahman's relationship to the world, while only twenty-seven affirm Identity, and all of these do so in a manner that reflects a Difference-in-Identity perspective in which the reality of the world is acknowledged.

Bādarāyaṇa's emphasis on the element of Difference is expressed in a variety of ways. As indicated above in our analysis of *sūtra* 1.1.1, the assertion that there is an inquiry into the Brahman implies the existence of a difference between an inquiring subject and the object to which the inquiry is directed. This same duality is reflected in 1.3.26 to 38, where Bādarāyaṇa presents an extended discussion on who is qualified to study the Vedas and achieve knowledge of the Brahman. While a non-dualist such as Śaṅkara can argue that this duality is 'real' only when perceived from a lower and ultimately invalid perspective, Bādarāyaṇa himself does not acknowledge the existence of such a distinction in two levels of knowledge. Nowhere does Bādarāyaṇa assert or even remotely hint that any of the positions expressed in his *sūtras* are meant to be interpreted as 'relatively' true but ultimately inaccurate. If, as is the intent of this work, we take Bādarāyaṇa's assertions at their face value, we must accept that the difference between the Brahman and the world which they express is intended by Bādarāyaṇa to be interpreted in a non-relative sense.

The role of Difference in Bādarāyaṇa's theology is also brought out through his emphasis on the Brahman as creator and sustainer of the world. As seen in our analysis of *sūtra* 1.1.2, Bādarāyaṇa begins his work by defining the Brahman in terms of his role as creator, sustainer, and destroyer of the world, thereby asserting the Difference that must in some sense exist between the creator and his creation. That Bādarāyaṇa would place this definition of the Brahman at such a crucial point as the beginning of his entire work would suggest that he understood it as an essential definition of the Brahman, and therefore we must also conclude that Bādarāyaṇa understood the creator–creation difference to be an essential, and perhaps *the* essential, aspect of the relationship between Brahman and the world. The significance of the creator/creation duality is further reflected throughout the *Brahma Sūtras* as Bādarāyaṇa repeatedly interprets topical texts by pointing out that the passage in question must refer to the Brahman because of the presence of qualities associated with creating or sustaining the world. Likewise, he proves that passages do *not* refer to the individual soul because of the presence of these same qualities. This is found in not only the first chapter, but other chapters of the *Brahma Sūtras* as well. Throughout the work, creating and sustaining the world is seen as an attribute of the Brahman that reflects His greatness and distinguishes Him from the far less powerful individual soul.

The element of Difference is also apparent from the fact that in most of the *sūtras*, Bādarāyaṇa attempts to demonstrate that a passage refers to the Brahman, and not to a soul, god, or the world. In other words, Bādarāyaṇa is repeatedly affirming that some type of Difference exists between the Brahman and the world each time he argues that a passage applies to the Brahman and not to any other reality. In fact, much of the first chapter can be seen as an attempt to affirm the greatness of the Brahman in contrast to the lesser qualities of His creation. Thus, we see such qualities as creatorship, freedom from sin, invisibility, and possessing a divine form attributed to the Brahman only, thereby affirming a Difference between Him and the world which lacks such qualities. We might add that this also indicates that Bādarāyaṇa understood the Brahman as a being possessing qualities, in contrast to Śaṅkara's understanding of the

Brahman as pure, unqualified intelligence.

With reference to those *sūtras* which assert some type of Identity, in each case the Identity is presented in terms of immanence in which the Brahman dwells within a world which retains its own reality. The Brahman's immanent presence does not negate the reality of the physical universe or the soul. Rather, all are real, with the Brahman dwelling in the soul and the physical universe as the power which creates and sustains them. Thus, Bādarāyaṇa describes the Brahman in terms such as residing in the heart (1.2.7–8), the person in the eye and the sun (1.2.13–17), the inner controller (1.2.20), and the being who dwells in the space in the heart (1.3.14–21). Clearly these *sūtras* affirm an element of Identity, but it is equally clear that they acknowledge the existence of the realities in which the Brahman dwells, thus affirming an element of Difference alongside the elment of Identity. That Difference is affirmed also can be seen from the fact that in all of the above *sūtras*, Bādarāyaṇa explicitly states that the subject in question is *not* the individual soul. Indeed, throughout the first chapter, Bādarāyaṇa is found to repeatedly declare that certain passages do not refer to the individual soul, and do refer to the Brahman, and by doing so Bādarāyaṇa certainly must be operating from a position that perceives the Brahman and the soul to be different.

There are further indications in the first chapter that Bādarāyaṇa's understanding of Identity includes a recognition of the reality of the created world, and hence a recognition of Difference. Thus, in the description of three types of Identity between the Brahman and the soul, found in 1.4.20–22, the reality of the soul clearly is assumed in each case. Furthermore, when Bādarāyaṇa closes the fourth part of the first chapter with a discussion of the Brahman as both material and efficient cause, he thereby affirms that the Brahman shares some type of identity with His creation since He is its material cause, but at the same time it is different from the created world since He and He alone is the being who creates the world, in contrast to the other real but less powerful parts of his creation.

THE THEOLOGY OF THE BRAHMA SŪTRAS: A SUMMARY OF CHAPTERS TWO, THREE, AND FOUR

While the scope of this work has been limited to an analysis of the first chapter of the *Brahma Sūtras*, it should be noted, without engaging in a similarly detailed analysis, that the theology found in the three remaining chapters is consistent with that which we have found in Chapter One. The emphasis is on the Brahman as intimately present within His creation, but nonetheless different from and superior to that creation which is real.

This theological perspective is seen in Bādarāyaṇa's tendency to continue to describe the Brahman in terms of His role as creator, thus reinforcing our belief expressed in the analysis of 1.1.2 that the Brahman's role as creator is its essential quality, according to Bādarāyaṇa. We see that section 2.1 focuses on His role as creator through a lengthy analysis of the nature of the cause/effect relationship, an analysis which affirms both Difference and Identity. Section 2.2. evaluates different theories of creation, including those found in Atomism and Jainism. The overall intent of this section affirms that the created world is real, but that the Brahman is not separated from the created world. Creation continues to be a prominent subject in sections 2.3 and 2.4.

The element of Difference is also brought out in Bādarāyaṇa's frequent declarations on the nature of the individual soul, in which it is described as less than the Brahman in a variety of ways. *Sūtra* 2.3.17 begins a lengthy section on the nature of the individual soul, in which Bādarāyaṇa affirms that it possesses such qualities as being atomic, a part, and an agent. Perhaps most significantly, Bādarāyaṇa also declares that the individual soul is completely dependent for its existence on the independent Brahman, thereby asserting a crucial difference that is also regarded as central to the theologies of Madhva, Rāmānuja, and Nimbārka. The limited qualities of the individual soul are also contrasted with the pure and perfect nature of the Brahman. That a differnece of some type exists between the Brahman and the individual soul is also reflected in Bādarāyaṇa's extensive discussion of the departure of the soul from the body, the path it follows, and the process of rebirth, as found in sections 3.1, 3.2, 4.2, and 4.3. In all of these sections, Bādarāyaṇa's thoughts only make sense if one assumes that the soul exists as a being which in some sense is separate from the Brahman; in a system of pure Identity, it would be nonsensical to talk about a soul pursuing a path to an ultimate goal, since in reality they would be one.

In a similar manner, the element of Difference is reflected in the sections of the *Brahma Sūtras* in which Bādarāyaṇa discusses the means of attaining the Brahman. Thus, in sections 3.3., 3.4, and 4.1,

Bādarāyaṇa examines the various issues pertaining to the means by which the individual soul achieves its ultimate goal of liberation from the finite world and union with the Brahman. Again, such a discussion only makes sense if one assumes the existence of a seeker and the object sought.

Śaṅkara, of course, argues that such discussions are presented at the lower level of knowledge where Difference is falsely believed to be real, when in truth there is only the one undifferentiated Brahman. However, as we have pointed out several times already, Bādarāyaṇa makes no such statement: he does not qualify his remarks by passing them off as only true in a relative sense, and hence if we are to let Bādarāyaṇa speak for himself we must accept his statements at face value, including their many references to the Difference between the Brahman and His creation.

This is not to say, of course, that chapters two, three and four of the *Brahma Sūtras* do not contain any passages which describe some type of Identity between the Brahman and the world. Such passages exist, but they are the exception rather than the rule, and they describe a type of Identity which can contain Difference within it. Thus, for example, *sūtra* 4.1.3 refers to viewing the Brahman as oneself (*Ātmeti*) when meditating. Similarly, we find the word 'non-division' (*avibhāgaḥ*) used in 4.2.16 to describe the union of the individual soul and the Brahman after the soul's death. The same word is used in 4.4.4 to describe the released soul. But when these apparent references to Identity are looked at in the context of the rest of the *Brahma Sūtras*, it is readily apparent that Bādarāyaṇa must be referring to a type of Identity in which Difference is present. Thus, after describing the 'non-division' of the Brahman and the individual soul in 4.4.4, in the following *sūtra* Bādarāyaṇa describes the qualities of the released soul, implying that the soul maintains some type of separate existence even in the state of release. Bādarāyaṇa even points out that the released soul differs from the Brahman in at least one very crucial respect, in that the soul does not possess the power of creation, even in release.

CLOSING REMARKS

Based on our analysis of the first chapter of the *Brahma Sūtras*, we can say with considerable assurance that Bādarāyaṇa intended to present a theology of Difference-in-Identity, in which both the

Brahman and the world are real and distinct entities, yet at the same time intimately related in such a way that the world cannot exist apart from the Brahman. As the pure, all-powerful, perfect creator, the Brahman differs from the creation which is characterized by limitation in power and immersion in the world of change, impurity, and ignorance. The Brahman and the world stand related to each other as creator/creation, independent reality/ dependent reality, object of knowledge/seeker of knowledge, controlling reality/controlled reality. Through these categories, Bādarāyaṇa's theology reflects the doctrines of Realism and Difference, in that the Brahman and the world are depicted as distinct entities, each real, but one in a subordinate relationship to the other. At the same time, the element of Identity is also asserted in Bādarāyaṇa's theology through the doctrines of the Brahman as material cause of the world, and the Brahman residing within the world and controlling it from within. The Brahman and the world are distinct realities, but the Brahman is immanent within the world. Hence, we might characterize Bādarāyaṇa's theology as 'Immanent Realism'.

With reference to the major expositors, Bādarāyaṇa's theology clearly is far removed from that of Śaṅkara. Nowhere does Bādarāyaṇa deny the reality of the world and its individual souls. Nowhere does Bādarāyaṇa state, or even hint, that the many statements describing the Brahman and the world as distinct and real entities are meant to be understood as true in only a relative sense and ultimately false.

However, while Bādarāyaṇa's difference from Śaṅkara is easy to demonstrate, it is more difficult to determine which of the other expositors his theology more closely resembles. The themes of creation, dependence/independence, the reality of the world, and the purity of the Brahman are found in the theologies of many expositors, including Rāmānuja, Nimbārka, Vallabha, and even the dualist, Madhva. These theologies differ, in large part, on the basis of their *specific* explanations of the manner in which the Brahman and the world are related to eah other. In Bādarāyaṇa's theology, no such specific explanations are given: in essence, Bādarāyaṇa simply states that the Brahman creates the world and rules it from within, without defining the precise nature of that relationship. The detailed theologies of the expositors can be seen as their own creative and ingenious attempts to depict the Brahman-world relationship, but they cannot be seen as Bādarāyaṇa's own theology.

Bibliography

Agrawal, Madan Mohan. *The Philosophy of Nimbārka*. Gali Manihar: Shrimati Usha Agrawal, 1977.

Annangaracharyar, Śri Kanchi, ed. *Śrīmadvedāntadeśikagranthamālā*. Conjeevaram: Grathamala Office, 1940.

Banerjee, Nikunja. *The Spirit of Indian Philosophy*. New Delhi: Arnold-Heinemann, 1974.

Berry, Thomas. *Religions of India: Hinduism, Yoga, Buddhism*. New York: Bruce Publishing Company, 1971.

Bhandarkar, R.G. *Vaiṣṇavism, Śaivism, and Minor Religious Systems*. Varanasi: Reneshwar Singh, 1965.

Bhatt, S.R. *Studies in Rāmānuja Vedāanta*. New Delhi: Heritage Publishers, 1975.

Bishop, Donald H. *Indian Thought: An Introduction*. New York: Wiley and Sons, 1973.

Carmen. John. *The Theology of Rāmānuja: An Essay in Inter-religious Understanding*. New Haven: Yale University Press, 1974.

Chaudhuri, Haridas. "The Concept of Brahman in Hindu Religion." *Philosophy East and West* 4 (April 1954): 47–66.

Chettimattam, John B. *Consciousness and Reality: An Indian Approach to Metaphysics*. Mary Knoll, New York: Orbis Books, 1971.

Das Gupta, Surendranath. *A History of Indian Philosophy*. 5 vols. Cambridge: University Press, 1949.

Edgerton, Franklin. *The Beginnings of Indian Philosophy*. Cambridge: Harvard University Press, 1965.

Edgerton, Franklin, trans. *The Bhagavad Gītā*. Cambridge; Harvard University Press, 1972.

Farquhar, J.N. *An Outline of the Religious Literature of India*. Delhi: Motilal Banarsidass, 1920.

Garge, Damodar. *Citations in Śabara-Bhāṣya*. Poona: Deccan College, 1952.

Ghate, V.S. *The Vedānta: A Study of the Brahma Sūtras with the Bhāṣyas of Śaṅkara, Rāmānuja, Nimbārka, Madhva, and Vallabha*. Poona: Bhandarkar Oriental Research Institute, 1960.

Hayavadana, Rao, ed. *The Śrīkara Bhāṣya: Being the Viraśaiva Commentary on the Vedānta Sūtras of Śripati*. Bangalore: Bangalore Press, 1936.

Hiriyana, M. *The Essentials of Indian Philosophy*. London: George Allen and Unwin, Ltd., 1949.

Hopkins, Thomas J. *The Hindu Religious Tradition*. Encino, California: Dickenson Publishing Company. 1971.

Hume, Robert E., trans. *The Thirteen Principal Upaniṣads*. London; Oxford University Press, 1977.

Joshi, C.N. *The Evolution of the Concepts of Ātman and Mokṣa in the Different Systems of Indian Philosophy*. Ahmedabad: Gujarat University. 1965.

Keith, A.B. *The Religion and the Philosophy of the Vedas and the Upaniṣads*. Harvard Oriental Series, Vol. 32. Cambridge: Harvard University Press, 1925.

Kumarappa, Bharatan. *The Hindu Conception of Deity as Culminating in Rāmānuja*. London: Luzac and Co., 1934.

Lester, Robert. "Rāmānuja and Śri Vaiṣṇavism: The Concept of Prapatti or Sarangati." *History of Religions* 5 (Winter 1966). 266–282.

Lott, Eric J. *God and the Universe in the Vedantic Theology of Rāmānuja: A Study in His Use of the Self-body Analogy*. Madras: Rāmānuja Research Society. 1976.

Madhva. *The Chāndogya Upaniṣad with Commentary*. Śrisa Vasu, trans. B.D. Basu, ed. Vol. 3 of *Sacred Books of the Hindus*. New York: AMS Press, 1974.

Marfatia, Mrudula. *The Philosophy of Vallabha*. Delhi: Munshiram Manoharlal, 1967.

Mishra, Umesha. *The Nimbārka School of Vedānta*. Allahabad: Tirabhukti Publications, 1966.

Monier-Williams, Monier. *A Sanskrit-English Dictionary*. Delhi: Motilal Banarsidass, 1989.

Narain, K. *An Outline of Madhva Philosophy*. Allahabad: Udayana Publications, 1962.

Padmanabhacharya, C.M. *The Life and Teachings of Śri Madhvacharya*. Udipi: Paryaya Sri Palimar Mutt n.d.

Pereira, Jose. "*Bādarāyana: Creator of Systematic Theology*". *Religious Studies* 22 (February 1987): 193–204.

Pereira, Jose, ed. *Hindu Theology: A Reader*. Garden City: Image Books, 1976.

Radhakrishnan, Sarvepalli. *The Brahma Sūtra: The Philosophy of Spiritual Life*. London; George Allen and Unwin Ltd. 1960.
Radhakrishnan, Sarvepalli. *Indian Philosophy*. Two vols. New York; MacMillan Co., 1927.
Raju, P.T. *Structural Depths of Indian Thought*. Albany: State University of New York Press, 1985.
Sen Gupta, Anima. *A Critical Study of the Philosophy of Rāmānuja*. Varanasi: Chowkhamba Sanskrit Series Office. 1967.
Shah, Jethalal. *Śri Vallabha: His Philosophy and Religion*. Gujarat: Pustimargiya Pusatakalya, 1969.
Sharma, B.N.K. *A History of the Dvaita School of Vedanta and its Literature*. Two vols. Bombay: Booksellers, 1960.
Sharma, B.N.K. *Madhva's Teachings in His Own Words*. Bombay: Bharatiya Vidya Bhavan, 1979.
Sharma, B.N.K. *The Brahma Sūtras and Their Principal Commentaries*. 3 vols. Bombay: Bharatiya Vidya Bhavan, 1971.
Sharma, Chandradhar. *Indian Philosophy: A Critical Survey*. New York; Barnes and Noble, 1962.
Sharma, I.C. *Ethical Philosophies of India*. Lincoln: Johnsen Publishing Co., 1965.
Sinha, Jadunath. *The Philosophy of Nimbārka*. Calcutta: Sinha Publishing House, 1973.
Thibaut, George, trans. *The Vedānta Sūtras of Bādarāyaṇa with the Commentary of Rāmānuja*. Delhi: Motilal Banarsidass, 1962. Reprint of *Sacred Books of the East*, v. 48.
Thibaut, George, trans. *The Vedānta Sūtras of Bādarāyaṇa with the Commentary of Śaṅkara*. Two vols. New York: Dover, 1962. Reprint of *Sacred Books of the East*, v. 38.
Van Buitenen, J.A.B. *Rāmānuja on the Bhagavad Gītā*. Delhi: Motilal Banarsidass, 1968.
Walker, Benjamin. *The Hindu World*. Two vols. New York: Frederick Praeger, 1968.
Zaehner, R.C., trans. *The Bhagavad Gītā*. London: Oxford University Press, 1969.
Zaehner, R.C., trans. *Hindu Scriptures*. New York. E.P. Dutton and Co., 1966.

Appendix A: A Comparison of Adhikaraṇa and Sūtra Breakdowns

ADHIKARAṆAS

EXPOSITOR	1.1	1.2	1.3	1.4	2.1	2.2	2.3	2.4	3.1	3.2	3.3	3.4	4.1	4.2	4.3	4.4	TOTAL
Śaṅkara	11	7	13	8	13	8	17	9	6	8	36	17	14	11	6	7	191
Rāmānuja	11	6	11	8	10	8	7	8	6	8	25	15	11	11	5	6	156
Madhva	12	7	14	7	11	12	19	13	20	20	42	11	8	10	6	11	223

SUTRAS

EXPOSITOR	1.1	1.2	1.3	1.4	2.1	2.2	2.3	2.4	3.1	3.2	3.3	3.4	4.1	4.2	4.3	4.4	TOTAL
Śaṅkara	31	32	43	28	37	45	53	22	27	41	66	52	19	21	16	22	555
Rāmānuja	32	33	44	29	34	42	52	19	27	40	64	51	19	20	15	22	543
Madhva	31	32	43	28	38	45	53	23	29	42	68	51	19	22	16	23	563

Appendix B: An Analysis of Sūtra Length

Below is a breakdown of the number of words in the *sūtras* of the first chapter of the *Brahma Sūtras*. The top left hand columns count the total number of words in the *sūtra*. The top right hand columns count the number of essential words per *sūtra*, eliminating conjunctions, adverbs, and other words that do not contribute significantly to the translation. The bottom columns count the number of compounds per *sūtra*.

Total Words	Number of Sūtras	Total Essential Words	Number of Sūtras
1	3	1	14
2	18	2	40
3	29	3	34
4	28	4	29
5	20	5	10
6	13	6	3
7	9	7	2
8	4	8	1
9	2	9	0
10	3	10	1
11	1		
12	0		
13	2		
14	1		
15	1		

Number of Compounds	Number of Sūtras
1	33
2	42
3	23
4	18
5	5
6	8
7	4
8	0
9	1

Appendix C: Bādarāyaṇa's Methodology

Bādarāyaṇa employs at least six different techniques for demonstrating the truth of his propositions. Below is a list of the techniques used by Bādarāyaṇa, the number of times that each technique is used in 1.1, and a list of the *sūtras* in which each technique is found.

Technique	Times used	Sūtras
1. Proof by reference to the Brahman's qualities	25	1.1.16, 1.1.20, 1.1.22, 1.1.28, 1.2.2, 1.2.3, 1.2.12, 1.2.13, 1.2.14, 1.2.17, 1.2.18, 1.2.19, 1.2.21, 1.3.3, 1.3.9, 1.3.10, 1.3.11, 1.3.13, 1.3.15, 1.3.16, 1.3.18, 1.3.39, 1.3.40, 1.3.41, 1.4.16
2. Proof by reference to context	5	1.1.29, 1.2.10, 1.3.6, 1.4.5, 1.4.19
3. Proof by reference to symbolic language.	4	1.1.25, 1.2.7, 1.2.26, 1.3.21
4. Proof by appeal to Scripture	9	1.1.4, 1.1.10, 1.1.11, 1.2.6, 1.2.25, 1.3.23, 1.3.30, 1.3.38, 1.4.25
5. Proof by appeal to general knowledge	2	1.2.1, 1.3.17
6. Proof by reference to other authorities	9	1.2.28, 1.2.29, 1.2.30, 1.2.31, 1.3.31, 1.4.18, 1.4.20, 1.4.21, 1.4.22

INDEX

Abundance (*bhūman*), 89-90, 127
Adhikaraṇa, 12-13
Adhyāya, 12
Aditi, 72
Agni, 74
Aitareya Upaniṣad, 63
Ajātaśatru, 115
Akṣara, 91
Aṇubhāṣya, 29
Anyatraivaprasiddha, 46
Anyatraprasiddha, 46
Apauruseya, 42
Asat, 114
Āśmarathya, 11, 80-83, 117, 118
Ātreya, 11
Auḍulomi, 11, 117, 119
Avirodha, 12, 44-45
Avyakta, 107-10

Bādarāyaṇa, predecessors of, 10-11
Bādari, 11, 82
Baladeva, 19, 51
Bālāki, 115
Being (*sat*), 30, 47, 49, 92, 114
Bhāgavad Gītā, 7-8, 29, 32-33, 67, 70, 94-95
Bhāgavata Purāṇa, 27, 29, 32
Bhakti, 26-28, 31
Bhāskara, 19, 38
Bhūman see Abundance, 89-90, 127
Bliss, 90
Brahman 92
    Creator, 25-26, 28-30, 33-34, 37, 40-43, 48-50, 51-52, 54, 56, 57, 65-67, 70-71, 96-97, 99-100, 110-11, 113-17, 119-22, 129-33
    Forms (two), 94
    Knowledge of, 37
    Inquiry into, 14-15, 38-41
    Personal nature, 25-26, 28, 92, 110
    Qualities of, 20, 34, 50, 51, 53, 55, 58-59, 65, 67, 69, 73-74, 76-77, 78, 89, 114, 116, 127, 129-30
    Unqualified, 51
Brahmaṇas, 10
Brahma Sūtras
    Dating, 7-9
    Importance, 1-3
    Interpreting, problems of, 13-17, 127
    Structure of, 12-13, 42, 51-53, 108
Bṛeath, 60, 62-63, 103-04, 105, 116
Brightness, 111-12
Bṛhadāraṇyaka Upaniṣad, 16-17, 24, 47-48, 50, 58, 63, 64, 75, 76, 78, 91-92, 93, 105, 111-13, 117-18
Buddhist, 28

Caitraratha, 102-3
Categories, Sāṅkhyan, 112-13
Causality, types of, 30
    Efficient, 120-22
    Material, 120-22, 134
Cave, person in, 72-73
Chāndogya Upaniṣad, 47-49, 50, 58-61, 67, 69, 73-75, 79-81, 88-89, 93-95, 100-3, 104-5, 117, 120-21
Chariot, metaphor of, 107, 109
Christianity, 44
Cit (consciousness), 30
Concord (*Avirodha*), 12, 45-46

Darkness, 111
Das Gupta, Surendranath, 8
Deep sleep, 105
Desire, 57
Devotion (*bhakti*), 26-27, 28-29, 31, 34
Dharma, 9, 31
Difference, 33-34, 40, 42, 44-45, 56-59, 65, 70-72, 75, 77-78, 83, 87-88, 90, 92, 96, 101, 105, 110, 118, 122, 129-34

Difference in Identity, 57, 70-73, 83, 96, 129-34
Dramida, 23
Dualism, 31

Eater, 71
Edgerton, Franklin, 7
Efficient cause, 120-22, 131
Emanation, 120-21
Ether, 74
Eye, person in, 73-75, 131

Fire
  Deity, 80-96
  Element, 80-82
Form (and name), 98, 100, 104-5
Fruit (*phalam*), 12

Garg, Damodar, 9
Gargi, 91, 93
Gauḍapāda, 20
Gautama, 102
Gāyatrī, 60-62
Ghate, 4, 96, 119
Gītābhāṣya, 23
Gods, 98-101
Govinda, 20
Grace, 29, 31, 34-35
Great (*mahat*), 108, 110

Heart
  Person in, 68, 70, 131
  Small space in, 93-97, 104-05, 127
Heaven, 62
Hell, 35
Hiraṇyagarbha, 35
Honey, knowledge, 99, 100, 111-12

Identity, 57-58, 62, 64-65, 69-70, 75, 78, 82, 83, 90, 96, 110, 117, 119, 121, 129-34
Imperishable (*akṣara*), 91-92
Indra, 62-64
Inexpressible, 47, 50
Inner Controller (*antaryāmin*), 24, 75-77, 131
Invisible, 78
Islam, 44

Jābālas, 81, 82-83, 103
Jaimini, 8, 9-10, 39, 80, 82-83, 99, 115-16
Jānaśruti, 101-2
Jñāna, 9
Jñānakāṇḍa, 10
Joy, 30, 53-54, 56
Judaism, 44

Kalpa Sūtras, 9
Kaṇvas, 76, 77, 113
Karma, 9, 38, 87, 116
Karmakāṇḍa, 9, 38
Kārṣṇājini, 11
Kāśakṛtsna, 11, 117, 119
Kaṭha Upaniṣad, 17, 47, 50, 71-72, 97, 103-4, 107-10
Kauṣītaki Upaniṣad, 62-63, 115
Kevalādvaita, 20, 32
Knowledge, 9
Kṛṣṇa, 27, 28-29, 31
Kṣatriya, 102
Kumārila Bhaṭṭa, 9

Light, 60-62, 99, 101, 104, 105, 111-12
Lingātmaka, 46
Lord, 105, 110

Madhva, 11, 12, 16-17, 19, 31-35, 39, 40, 41, 43, 46, 48, 49, 52, 54, 58, 61, 63-64, 68, 71-72, 73, 75, 77, 81, 82-83, 86-87, 89-90, 92, 96, 108-9, 111, 116, 132
Madhyandins, 76, 77, 113
Mahat, 108, 110
Maitreyi, 117-18
Manifestation (*āvirbhāva*), 30
Manu, 64
Manu Smṛti, 102
Material Cause, 120-22, 131, 134
Māyā, 21, 29-30
Methodologies, 40, 126-28
Mīmāṁsā, 9
Mīmāṁsā Sūtras, 8, 39

Mind, 67, 69
Monier-Williams, 38, 119
Muṇḍaka Upaniṣad, 48, 78-79, 85-87, 117, 121

Nāmātmaka, 46
Name (and form), 98, 100, 104-5
Nimbārka, 19, 27-29, 38, 40, 49, 50, 51, 70-72, 75, 77, 103-4, 108, 132, 134
Non-being (*asat*), 114
Non-dualism, Qualified, 23, 34, 42, 76

Om, 92
Order (*Samanvaya*), 12, 37, 83

Pādas, 12-13
Pain, 70
Paratantra, 33
Paratantrya, 27
Pariṇāma, 20, 25, 28, 122
Passion, 111
Pereira, Jose, 14, 16, 23, 27, 31, 34
Person,
  In the cave, 72-73
  In the eye, 73-74, 131
  In the heart, 68, 70, 131
  In the sun, 58
  Size of the thumb, 97-98, 103-4
Phalam, 12
Pleasure, 68, 70
Potter/clay metaphor, 120, 121
Prabhākara, 9
Pramāṇas, 26, 32
Praśna Upaniṣad, 17, 50, 74, 92, 121
Pravṛtta Saṃhita, 17
Prime Matter, 15, 33, 46-50, 51-52, 57, 76-78, 85, 86-88, 91-92, 107-13
Purāṇas, 32
Puruṣa, 49, 109, 118
Pūrva Mīmāṃsā, 9, 10, 14, 28
Pūrvapakṣa, 44, 59

Qualified Non-dualism, 23, 34, 42, 76
Qualities, accidental, 41
Qualities, of Brahman. *See* Brahman

Radhakrishnan, S., 4, 45
Raikva, 101-2
Rāmānuja, 15, 17, 19-20, 22-27, 38, 40, 42, 44, 48-49, 50-51, 57-58, 62, 64, 68, 70-72, 75, 77, 81, 82-83, 86-87, 89-90, 92, 96, 97, 100, 103, 105, 108, 109, 111-12, 114, 115-16, 119, 121-22, 126, 134
Realism, 43, 122, 128, 131, 134
Release, 50
Ṛg Veda, 17, 33, 50

Śabara, 9
Sacrifice, 100
Sākṣi-jñāna, 33
Sākṣin, 33
Salvation,
  Means of, 26, 28, 31, 125, 132-33
  Nature of, 27, 28, 31, 35, 57, 125
Samanvaya, 12, 37, 83
Saṃhītas, 9
Śaṅkara, 12, 15-17, 19-23, 38-43, 46, 48-54, 56-58, 62, 64, 68, 70, 73, 75, 77, 79, 81-83, 89-90, 92, 96, 101, 103-6, 108-9, 111-12, 114-16, 119, 121-22, 126, 129-30, 133, 134
Sāṅkhya, 15, 38, 48-49, 52, 54, 76-77, 107-14, 118
Sāṅkhya-karika, 7
Sanskrit, 16-17
Śatapatha Brāhmaṇa, 102
Scripture, 43-45, 46-47, 55
Self (*Ātman*), 47, 50, 54, 56-57, 63, 73, 81, 86, 105, 113-14, 117-19
Sharma, B.N.K., 4, 7, 19
She-goat, 110-12
Smṛti, 70, 82, 94, 102, 128
Snake, metaphor of, 28, 33
Soul (*jīva*), 24, 26, 28, 30-31, 34, 47-48, 50, 54, 56, 58, 63, 67-72, 74-78, 85-87, 89, 90, 91, 92–97, 104-5, 115-16, 118-19, 129-33
Soul-body analogy, 24, 76
Sound, 14, 44
Space, 59, 95, 96, 104-5, 108
Specific, doctrine of, 34

Śrautasūtra, 8
Śrībhāṣya, 23
Śrīkaṇṭha, 19, 38
Śripati, 19
Subodhinī, 29
Substance-attribute, 24-25
Subtle body, 107, 109
Śuddhādvaita, 29
Śudras, 101-3
Śuka, 19
Sun, person in, 57-58
Support of universe, 85, 87-88, 93, 96
Śureśvara, 8
Sūtras, 12-18
Svābhāvika, 27
Svatantra, 33
Svātantṛya, 27
Śvetāśvatara Upaniṣad, 104, 111

Taittirīya Upaniṣad, 53-54, 56, 58, 114, 120, 122
Taṅka, 23
Tarka, 22
Theism, 92, 105, 110
Thumb, person size of, 97-98, 103-4
Tirobhāva, 30
Topical text, 12, 16-17, 51, 56, 59
Trembling, 104
Truth, levels of, 22, 26, 40, 42, 56, 71, 79, 96, 106, 129, 133
Two birds in tree, 86, 87

Ubhayatraprasiddha, 46
Unborn female, 110-11
Unmanifest (*avyakta*), 107-10
Upaniṣads, 1-2, 32; see *Aitereya; Bṛhadāraṇyaka; Chāndogya; Kaṭha; Kauṣitāki; Muṇḍaka; Praśna; Śvetāśvatara; Taittirīya*
Upāsanā, 27
Uttara Mīmāṁsā, 9-10, 32

Vaiśvānara, 79-83
Vājasaneyins, 81, 82-83, 115
Vallabha, 19, 29-31, 37, 134
Vāmadeva, 64
Vāyu, 32
Vedāntadeśika, 40
Vedāntadīpa, 23
Vedārthasaṃgraha, 23
Vedas, 32-33, 98-103
Vijñānabhikṣu, 19
Viṣaya vākya, 12, 16-17, 51
Viṣṇu, 28
Viṣṇu Purāṇa, 80
Vivarta, 20, 25
Vṛtti-jñāna, 33
Vyāpi-Vaikuntha, 31

Way (*Mārga*), 12
Witness, 33
Words, dual meaning of, 116
Works, 9, 22, 37-38, 39, 87, 116

Yādavaprakāśa, 19
Yājñavalkya, 91, 117-26
Yāmuna, 23
Yoga, 38
Yoga Sūtras, 7